D1080280

My HOLIDAYS

My HOLIDAYS

Sylvia Smith

PICADOR

First published 2003 by Picador
an imprint of Pan Macmillan Ltd
Pan Macmillan, 20 New Wharf Road, London N1 9RR
Basingstoke and Oxford
Associated companies throughout the world
www.panmacmillan.com

ISBN 0 330 41926 9

1 3 5 7 9 8 6 4 2

A CIP catalogue record for this book is available from
the British Library.

Typeset by Intype London Ltd
Printed and bound in Great Britain by
Mackays of Chatham plc, Chatham, Kent

I dedicate this, my third book, to my mother who knew of its existence but died one year before it was published. She used to say to me, 'I want to live long enough to see you rich and famous.'

Sylvia Smith

Quite a few of my holidays seem to be jinxed. When people ask me how I remember them in such detail, I reply, 'If you had experienced these holidays, surely you would remember them vividly too.' The holidays I don't remember are those that ran smoothly.

Occasionally I have altered the name of the person I travelled with or the name of the resort in an effort to eliminate embarrassment.

Sylvia Smith

Contents

My HOLIDAYS

one

Family Holidays

I was born in 1945, the only child of working-class parents, Reginald John and Lilian Violet Smith. We were a poor family with only my father working. He was employed as a skilled wireworker in a factory making fireguards and other wire-mesh items. Until I was aged twelve we lived in two rooms and a kitchen on the ground floor of a rented house in Walthamstow, East London. Another family lived upstairs and we shared the bathroom and back garden. We could not afford many holidays. I vaguely remember one at the age of six when we stayed in a boarding house in Margate, a seaside town on the south-east coast. I have a memory of sitting with ten other guests at a large dining table and being served boiled potatoes in their skins

3

soaked in butter. This was a novelty to me as my mother always peeled potatoes. I vaguely recall making sandcastles on the large beach and my father endeavouring to teach me to swim in the cold sea-water.

On Sundays during the summer we would travel by bus to Southend, a coastal town thirty miles outside London. My parents told me my first trip there was at the age of two. They took me to a huge firework display in the fairground at the end of the front. I was so frightened I hid under the bench we had been sitting on. My parents had to coax me out and take me outside.

I remember a trip to Southend at the age of eight. We had a three-course lunch in the restaurant of a hotel overlooking the grey sea. I was served jelly and ice cream and I found chinks of glass in the bowl. My father complained to the waitress and I was supplied with another jelly dessert. No thought was given to the possibility that I could have swallowed slivers of glass.

We would walk along Southend's mile-long pier, reputed to be the longest in the world, and along the front, playing bingo and trying the coconut shy in the varied amusement houses.

I was aged fourteen when my parents decided we

should have a second holiday, this time on the Isle of Wight, a small island off the south coast of England. We travelled on the ferry from the mainland to the island and boarded a train to Shanklin, a coastal town. My parents did not book accommodation. My father asked a taxi driver if he could recommend a boarding house. Fortunately the man's wife provided bed and breakfast in their home in the summer months so my father decided to look no further.

Our accommodation was clean and comfortable but we had to book a bath and were expected to make do with a washbasin every day. We spent pleasant days travelling around the island by bus and enjoyed walking along the cliffs from Shanklin to the neighbouring town of Sandown. Unfortunately we experienced typical English summer weather and it soon began to pour with rain. My father had to buy a mackintosh, and as he was only five foot three he was forced to buy the largest boy's size in a Shanklin department store. Despite the rain the weather was quite warm so my father and I chose to go swimming on Shanklin's beach. The sea was stormy and the waves were high and we thoroughly enjoyed swimming through them. A large wave caught my father and tossed him in the air. He landed flat on his back and just managed to grab his swimming trunks as the undercurrent pulled them and him down the sliding sand into the sea. Soon the weather improved and we were able to sunbathe in deckchairs on the beach. My mother was unable to swim and spent her time watching us. My father and I would change in and out of our swimwear on the beach, our bodies hidden by large bath towels. A lady sitting nearby walked over to my mother and handed her a pair of white knickers, asking, 'Do these belong to your daughter?' Unfortunately they did.

In my mid-teens all three of us were working, which enabled my parents to buy the rented house we were living in. A year later my grandfather died and his assets were sold. My father cleared the mortgage, booked a course of driving lessons and bought himself a brand-new car we named 'Nelly Belle' out of his inheritance. Every summer my parents would drive down the narrow roads to Cornwall in the west of England, encountering the lengthy traffic jams which were customary before the motorways were built. They purchased a small picnic stove, a tin kettle and some summer chairs and would have 'brew ups' in the lay-bys to break their journey, eating the sandwiches my mother had prepared earlier. When they arrived at the resort of their choice they would seek bed-and-breakfast accommodation, which was easily found. After an English breakfast each morning we would leave the house and we were not allowed to return until 10.30 p.m. at night, which I found to be completely unsatisfactory as I liked to freshen up and change my clothes after a day on the beach. We would travel over Cornwall's coastal roads to small fishing villages and would enjoy magnificent views of the cliffs, golden sands and the sea.

At the age of seventeen I began holidaying with my friends and would only accompany my parents occasionally on their yearly trips to Cornwall.

In my early twenties I joined my parents on their holiday. This time they toured Devon as well as Cornwall. We spent one night in Woolacombe, a coastal town nestling in the cliffs with an enormous beach spattered with jellyfish. We found bed-and-breakfast accommodation in a thatched house beside a church with a large cemetery. My room overlooked the graveyard. As I closed my curtains I noticed a sea mist swirling around the headstones. I was too frightened to sleep by myself so my mother spent the night with me in the double bed my room provided. At approximately 3 a.m. I had a nightmare and screamed at the top of my voice. My startled mother tried to placate me. We apologized for my mishap at breakfast later that morning. The landlady confirmed our suspicions that I had been overheard.

In my late twenties and thirties I had a long-standing boyfriend named Neil. He was six feet tall, blond, with sparkling blue eyes and a burly frame. He was two years younger than me. Neil and I decided to holiday with my parents, staying in Newquay, a seaside town in Cornwall. Once again my parents chose bed-and-breakfast accommodation whilst Neil and I booked into a guest house where we were free to come and go as we pleased. We joined my parents on day trips to Cornish fishing villages and also spent time sunbathing on Newquay's large beach, sitting in the harbour lazily watching the boats pass by. We had a pleasant holiday. On the journey home my father was stopped by the police for speeding. He was asked to get out of the car. As he didn't want to pay a fine my father tried to make friends with the policemen by pulling up the leg of his summer trousers, showing them he had a bad touch of sunburn on his shins. One of the policemen pointed out to him that he had the lives of three passengers in his hands.

My father apologized and was allowed to continue his journey with just a warning. That was the last holiday I spent with my parents.

On Sundays in the summer my parents would frequently motor down to Leysdown, a small coastal town in Kent, and park in a large car park overlooking the sea and have a picnic. One Sunday Neil and I joined them. Neil owned a rubber dinghy and decided to bring it along too. When we reached the car park my parents placed their miniature stove on the grass, made a cup of tea and got out the sandwiches. My mother and I left Neil and my father drinking tea whilst we walked into the town to play bingo in the amusement arcade. On our return we were surprised to see my father's clothing hanging over the doors of the car. As we approached the car we saw my father sitting in the driving seat wearing Neil's brown zip-up cardigan, with a tea towel placed over his private parts. We discovered that Neil had been rowing the dinghy in the sea whilst my father watched from a small jetty. My father asked if he could try out the dinghy. Neil climbed out of it as my father stepped into it. My father's foot completely missed the wooden centre panel and trod on the soft rubber, which resulted in the dinghy turning upside down and my father temporarily disappearing underneath the waves. My father took our laughter in his stride but it wasn't until we reached home that he told my mother and me precisely what he thought about Neil and his dinghy.

two
Shanklin, Isle of Wight
- 1962 -

Jean and I met when I became employed as an office junior for the same engineering company she worked for. We shared an office. She was short with mousy hair, slightly overweight and three years my senior. I was seventeen. We slowly became friends and would go to dances together on Saturday evenings. Jean was a smoker and would throw cigarettes onto my desk several times each day. I felt obliged to return them and would buy a packet from the company canteen. I soon became addicted to nicotine and my smoking days began.

Jean suggested we go on holiday together. I accepted her invitation. We scanned the pages of a daily newspaper and booked a two-week caravan holiday in the seaside town of Shanklin on the Isle of Wight. I was very excited as this would be my first holiday without my parents. My mother was not so pleased. My father told me: 'You've upset your mother because you don't want to go on holiday with us.'

Jean and I set off by train to Portsmouth harbour on the last Saturday in August, travelling on the ferry to the island. We eventually arrived at the caravan park, which sat on top of the cliffs. The park was very organized. It had its own clubhouse and a somewhat pricey supermarket. The showers and toilets were on the edge of a very muddy field. In those days caravans were equipped with kitchens and electricity only. Caravans containing shower rooms and toilets arrived some years later.

Jean and I spent most of our days travelling around the island by bus, visiting places of interest. The weather was a mixture of sunshine and showers but we did manage to sunbathe on the beach below the caravan site. We found the clubhouse filled with families with young children and very few available young men. So we would go to dances in town. We spent a few evenings in the caravan completing jigsaw puzzles. At the end of these evenings Jean would be desperate to urinate around 11 p.m. As the field was usually wet and muddy I chose to wait until morning before visiting the toilets. Jean was unable to wait and would don her walking shoes and stumble through the field in almost total darkness.

We visited Alum Bay and saw the famous Needles, which were several large rocks bursting from the sea. I remember we lost our way on the downs and walked several miles before discovering a town. We managed to find a bus stop and returned to Shanklin.

We would buy cigarettes daily from the supermarket and would pick up our mail. My parents wrote to me twice and enclosed sizeable banknotes for me to spend.

Late one evening we walked on Shanklin Pier and saw a sign inviting us to visit 'Madam Astra's' office and have our fortunes told. We thought that would be fun and walked towards the light shining behind the office. We discovered that Madam Astra's was closed and that the light belonged to a gents' toilet. The door was wide open revealing two men urinating. As they had their backs to us we walked away unnoticed, realizing they could be seen for some distance out at sea.

The second week of our holiday ran into

September. We saw a great exodus of families leaving the park for home. Few holidaymakers replaced them so the park was only one-quarter full.

Halfway through the second week Jean and I had a row. I decided the caravan needed a good clean but she didn't agree with me. An argument developed. Unfortunately Jean suffered from asthma. She was so upset she had a bad attack and spent half the night crying and trying to get her breath back. I tried to help her but she wouldn't speak to me. In the morning she seemed fine but she packed her suitcase and left for London, leaving me on my own for the last few days. I spent some time sightseeing but it was no fun by myself. I cleaned the caravan and then set off for London, one day earlier than I had intended.

I told my parents what had happened. I regretted my argument with Jean as we had been close friends. Several months passed. Then my father told me Jean's father had come to see me shortly after the holiday but I had been out shopping. He told my parents that Jean was very upset by the break up of our friendship and wanted to make amends. I was furious. I asked my father, 'Why didn't you tell me at the time?'

He replied, 'Well, we didn't think you would be interested.'

Jean did not return to the office after our holiday and by this time I had lost contact with her.

three
Utters, Austria
– 1963 –

Grace and I met when she became employed as a junior clerk for the same engineering company I worked for. We shared an office. Grace was very attractive. She had long black hair, a peaches-and-cream complexion and a shapely but slim figure. Grace and I decided to have a summer holiday overseas together. This would be the first time Grace and I had travelled abroad. With great excitement we leafed through the brochures we had obtained from a local travel agent. As our salaries were low we booked a two-week package holiday in a village called Utters in the Austrian Tyrol for the following July, travelling there and back midweek by coach. We made the booking in the January and spent the remaining months saving hard. A few weeks before our departure date we bought beautiful new clothing, none of it to be worn until our holiday.

We boarded the coach with the other holidaymakers at Victoria Coach Station and two hours later we were at the port of Dover. We leaned on the rail on the ferry and watched the white cliffs slowly fade out of sight. Fortunately it was good weather and we had a smooth crossing. We purchased various items in the duty-free shop, some drinks from the bar, and sat on deck enjoying our journey.

As we travelled through Belgium on the coach we stared out the windows at the unfamiliar countryside. Belgium seemed very flat. The coach stopped a few times for refreshments. Our final stop was Munich in picturesque Bavaria, Germany, where we had dinner. We slept fitfully and very uncomfortably overnight and drove through the mountains to arrive at our holiday resort the following morning.

We were given the key to our room, which was twin-bedded with a bathroom, and on the first floor. The hotel was typically Tyrolean with highly polished floorboards and large wooden chests acting as tables for freshly cut flowers in vases. Thick, fluffy white duvets laid on our beds to keep us warm overnight. We decided to unpack first, then shower, then go sightseeing.

Grace gave a gasp of horror and cried, 'Oh no! I don't believe it!'

I asked, 'What's the matter?' as Grace held up a brand-new orange day dress with a large dark stain around the waistline, which she had just removed from her suitcase. 'God!' I exclaimed. 'What's happened to that?'

Grace rummaged through her suitcase and eventually retrieved a polythene hair-lacquer bottle which was broken in two and completely empty. 'Oh no,' she cried. 'This lacquer bottle must have burst when the driver put my case in the boot with everyone else's. It's spilled all over everything and I haven't got a thing that isn't wet and sticky. Now what am I going to do?'

Grace washed her clothing in the basin in the bathroom, using the hotel soap, but the stains would not shift. She had packed six new summer dresses, a new pair of black trousers, a swimsuit and some tops. The dresses and tops were unwearable but the stains on the swimsuit and trousers hardly noticed. I said, 'Well, you can't live in trousers for two weeks so you'll have to borrow some of my things.' I had packed a total of sixteen outfits to make sure I had something suitable to wear for every occasion that might present itself. Eight of my dresses were brand new and I would not allow Grace to wear them. Instead I offered her a multicoloured cotton dress and jacket, two summer dresses and two blouses, all of which I had bought the previous year. Grace hated the dress and jacket and the other clothing was not to her taste either. She was also a size smaller than me so none of it was a perfect fit. But she had no choice other than to wear my clothes, as her 'spending money' would only just cover her daily expenses.

Lunch was between 1 and 2 p.m. and we managed to get to the dining hall on time. We noticed that the English tourists were seated on one side of the room and the German tourists on the other. The food was excellent. We returned to our room to freshen up with the intention of walking through the village. We climbed the stairs to the first floor. Grace walked across the hallway towards one of the bedrooms. I called out, 'Grace. Where are you going?' too late to prevent her from turning the handle and entering an unknown bedroom.

She returned to the hall blushing and exclaiming, 'I'm terribly sorry.'

I asked, 'What on earth happened there? Our room is at the end of the passage.'

Grace put her hand over her red face and said, 'God knows why I did that. I've never been so embarrassed in my life. The couple inside were having a bit of nookie. The woman was laying flat on her back on the bed with her legs apart. Her skirt was right over her head and she was naked from the waist down and the feller didn't have any clothes on at all. I just cannot tell you what they were doing.'

'Oh, Grace,' I exclaimed.

She laughed and said, 'They should have locked their door.'

The two concerned were members of our party and we were to see them every mealtime and on the homeward journey.

Grace and I had a leisurely walk through the village. It was surrounded by mountains but was small with just the one main street comprising a supermarket, a few shops and a cafe on one side, and a church and a graveyard, a travel bureau, a small mini-golf centre and a lake on the other, with approximately thirty houses scattered around it. Our hotel was on the edge of the village and was the only form of nightlife. Its bar was open until midnight each day and a Tyrolean evening was held every Saturday in the vast hall, which doubled as a dining room. The tourists were mainly English and German and we were all housed in the one large hotel. During our stroll we noticed a middle-aged English couple sitting on a bench at the foot of a mountain. The woman was occupied knitting a pale blue garment whilst her husband stared blankly ahead.

The travel bureau was actually a large log cabin, typical of those in the mountains. We went inside to see what day trips were on offer. We were served by a tall blond man aged about thirty-seven, who introduced himself as Rudi Meier. We exchanged names and after much discussion we booked a coach trip to northern Italy which departed two days later. Rudi was very friendly towards me and eventually asked, 'Can I take you to a nightclub this evening? I can bring a friend along for your friend.'

I looked at Grace, who shrugged her shoulders and said, 'All right. It might be fun.' We arranged to meet in the hotel bar at nine fifteen.

Grace and I busied ourselves getting ready for dinner at 8 p.m. and our date. I selected a low-cut blue dress from the wardrobe whilst Grace was forced to wear my dress and jacket as the other clothing I had loaned was not suitable. She grimaced and said, 'I hate the colours in this outfit and it's miles too big for me.' At dinner we were embarrassed to see a mother and her teenage daughter from our party sitting at the dining table with curlers in their wet hair.

At nine fifteen sharp Rudi entered the bar with a tall dark-haired man he introduced as Bernhardt. We all climbed into Rudi's Mercedes and he drove to a bar a few miles from the village. Rudi told us that he owned the travel bureau and the coach used for day trips and that he hoped to expand. He asked how old we were. Grace was seventeen but I had just turned eighteen. He joked that possibly we were too young to go to a nightclub and said he was twenty-seven. Neither Grace nor I believed him. After a few drinks and light conversation between the four of us Rudi drove to a club where we danced to the music of a live band. Bernhardt did not speak much English but Grace and he seemed to enjoy themselves.

During the course of the evening Rudi asked me to live with him, saying he would pay my fare home if things didn't work out. I was very flattered but I did not reply to his offer. The age of consent in the UK was twenty-one and I realized if I did not return home with the party then my father would appear the following day. I found Rudi to be very pleasant but he was far too old for me. At the end of the evening Grace told me she was not too keen on Bernhardt so they had not made any further dates.

Rudi would occasionally sit at the next table during lunchtime and we would talk but I think he found me too ladylike and unsophisticated for his tastes and his interest in me waned.

The morning after our date Grace and I rose very late and dashed to the dining room just in time for Continental breakfast and several cups of coffee. We decided to don swimsuits underneath trousers and go for a swim. The lake was crowded with English and German tourists lying on its grassy banks. Our swimming did not last very long as we found the bottom of the lake to be very muddy and we noticed water rats scuttling through the reeds. We dried ourselves with bath sheets and then endeavoured to change back into our trousers using the towels as shields. To our displeasure two young German men watched our every move.

The next day we had an early breakfast and boarded Rudi's coach for our trip to northern Italy. We drove along the winding mountain roads and saw spectacular views. Grace chose to sit by the

28

window but we soon changed places as the coach drove on the very edge of the road and she found this frightening. Also the continuous turning upset her stomach. We stopped in a typical north Italian town and were allotted four hours to sightsee. I went into a tobacconist to buy twenty cigarettes and was charged £1.50. I realized this was a sky-high price but in my youth I was too embarrassed to argue so I paid the requested amount. On the return journey Grace became very unwell. We reached the hotel shortly before dinnertime. Grace asked for a glass of milk and went to bed for the remainder of the evening, forgoing her meal. She spent the next day in bed feeling ill and didn't rise until dinnertime, when she consumed only a bowl of soup and a slice of bread.

Grace and I spent our days exploring the area and walking along mountain paths. One afternoon we boarded a cable car to take us to a restaurant at the top of a mountain. We booked another day trip with Rudi, this time travelling to Innsbruck, the capital of the Tyrol. Rudi took the opportunity to tell us our sandals were dangerous for climbing and we should have brought proper walking shoes. Despite this we had no accidents.

We examined the ornate Roman Catholic church

and admired its beautiful stained-glass windows. We noticed that even the cemetery was different to those at home as every grave had a coloured photograph of its occupant moulded into the tombstone.

The Tyrolean evenings were a great success. We thoroughly enjoyed watching the traditional dancers in their gay costumes and listening to the yodelling. After the floorshows we spent the remainder of both evenings dancing with the locals and the English and German tourists.

During one lunchtime two young German men from the other side of the dining room began making eyes at us. We smiled and waved at them. Using sign language they asked if we would like to spend the afternoon with them. We nodded in agreement. All four of us climbed into their Volkswagen Beetle car. My date was called Claus. He was the driver. I sat beside him as Grace shared the back seat with Helmut. Claus drove many miles through the Tyrol. He stopped at a huge lake surrounded by mountains. We sat outside a large cafeteria drinking tea, eating cake and enjoying the view. The four of us tried to converse with our meagre knowledge of each others' languages. We exchanged addresses and promised to write to one another as Claus and Helmut were at the end of their holiday and were returning to Germany that evening. (None of us ever did.)

The day before our return to the UK we bought sandwiches, fruit and orange juice from the village supermarket to eat on the journey home as we found the refreshment centres far too expensive.

The following morning we set off for London. Our first stop was Munich. Everyone left the coach to have lunch, leaving Grace and me inside with our sandwiches. After an hour had passed both Grace and I were in urgent need of a toilet. We tried to open the coach door only to find it was locked. In our desperation we had no choice but to urinate in the toilet at the back of the vehicle. Some twenty minutes later the two drivers and our party returned. A few kilometres along the autobahn Grace and I noticed a wide trail of urine trickling down the aisle, slowly making its way to the drivers' seats. Unfortunately all the other members of our party noticed it too. Soon there was much conversation and laughter. Grace said in a very loud voice, 'That was your fault! You didn't press the right button!'

As we turned a sharp corner, oranges and newspapers fell from the racks below the ceiling into the urine. All the occupants of the coach realized what had happened. A man further down the front called out, 'As it's raining hard I wonder if we're going to have snow next?' The co-driver slowly made his way along the aisle to flush the toilet. Despite my embarrassed amusement I made a silent vow never, ever again to use a coach lavatory.

The remainder of the journey home was un-eventful.

four
Paris, France
- 1966 -

Sophie and I met when I accepted employment with the same company of chartered accountants she worked for in the City. We were both shorthand secretaries to partners and shared an office. We slowly became friends. She was tall, slim and dark haired and twenty-two years old, one year older than me. We decided to have a ten-day package holiday in Paris in the summer.

On the departure date we joined the coach at Victoria Coach Station and were driven to Lydd Airport in Kent. We boarded a small aeroplane which carried thirty passengers. We chatted as we flew over the Channel and looked out the window over France to see a small airstrip below with sheep grazing on the grass beside the runway. We landed safely at Beauvais Airport. A second coach drove us to Paris.

Our hotel was in a side street of a poor area in Paris and was family run. Our room was on the first floor. The lift stopped halfway up the staircase and we had to climb the remaining stairs to our passageway. The room was shabbily furnished. Every time we opened the curtains they would fall down. When we climbed into the double bed we each rolled into a separate niche in the mattress. I opened the desk drawer to see the worn carpet as the drawer had no bottom to it. The bathroom was in the corridor and we shared it with all the other guests on our floor. During the course of the holiday I noticed the maid stole two packets of the cigarettes I had bought on the plane. Breakfast each day was simply croissants and a pot of coffee and the hotel did not cater for lunch or dinner. We accepted our plight with good humour.

Sophie and I spent our days shopping and seeing the sights, travelling on the Métro or on foot. Several times we lost our way and asked French passers-by for directions only to be totally ignored. We enjoyed the historic buildings, my favourite being the Sacré Cœur. We booked a coach trip to Versailles, the home of the French kings. We also entered a French hairdresser's with disastrous results. After dinner we would sometimes visit a bar and we found a French barman picking his nose to be a common sight. Both of us disliked the open men's toilets in the streets. They were frequently smelly.

We saw a disco advertised on the hotel notice board and asked the manager to telephone for a minicab to take us there. The cab driver was a young Italian who spoke fluent French and a little English. Sophie had a slight knowledge of French and they began talking to each other. Sophie kept me up to date with the conversation. He told us his name was Paolo and that his family had moved from Italy to Paris some years earlier. He did not recommend the disco we had chosen. Instead he asked if he could collect his younger brother Carlo from their home and suggested we all go to a nightclub, with Carlo being my date for the evening. We both agreed.

The brothers were in their twenties. Paolo was the older of the two. They were dark and attractive. We entered the nightclub of their choice and were shown to a table beside the dance floor. Paolo ordered our drinks. A small band played lively music on the edge of a stage. Sophie and I were astounded to see topless dancers appear. It was such a shock, coupled with the realization that we were obviously in a strip club, that we burst into uncontrollable laughter. The girls eventually finished their act which had consisted of jumping up and down and rotating their boobs whilst Sophie and I slowly regained our composure. The brothers asked us to dance on the crowded dance floor. Unfortunately a drunk and his partner accidentally collided with me and Carlo. Carlo swiftly slapped him around the face. The drunk responded with his fists and a fight broke out with Paolo joining in. Sophie and I dashed off the floor. Several tables were overturned and we were splashed with alcohol. Two bouncers were able to stop the fighting whilst the commissionaire collected our coats and escorted the four of us out of the club.

We returned to the car. Paolo drove us to a club owned by a friend of his. We were introduced to Pierre and seated at a table near the bar. Pierre produced a bottle of wine and some glasses. The three men spoke to each other in rapid French. In broken English Pierre suggested we should hear Carlo sing. Sophie and I politely smiled and nodded in agreement. Pierre picked up a guitar from behind the bar and began to strum it whilst Carlo looked into my eyes and sang in French. I didn't understand a word but I gathered it was a very passionate air as Carlo clenched his fists and banged them on the table and contorted his face, still looking me straight in the eye. I was extremely embarrassed and wondered how he could be so self-confident. I was grateful when the song ended.

In the early hours of the morning Paolo returned us to the hotel. Carlo asked if he could see me again. I replied, 'No.'

He hesitated and then snapped, 'Get out!' Sophie and I alighted from the car and entered the hotel.

Sophie and I spent a pleasant afternoon walking along the Champs-Élysées and looking through the windows of the famous fashion houses. We sat at a table outside one of the gay cafes eating cake and drinking coffee, watching endless traffic pass by. Late afternoon we photographed the famous Arc de Triomphe and returned to our hotel, travelling there by the Métro. We met two young GIs on the train, who walked us to our hotel. We exchanged names. Jay and Toni told us they were serving in the US Army based in Germany and were on three days' leave, and were due to return the next day. It was arranged that they would call for us at 9 p.m.

We waited in reception and, true to their word, our GIs arrived shortly before nine. They told us they had been recommended to a jazz club just off the Champs-Élysées. It was decided that we should go there. Jay was Sophie's date and Toni mine. We ordered a cab and twenty minutes later we arrived at the jazz club. The GIs paid our entrance fee and we sat at a table close to the bar. Toni ordered our drinks. The jazz club was excellent with a live band. We spent the evening listening to them and talking to our GIs. We had a second drink then the men told us they had no more money with them. Unfortunately Sophie and I hadn't thought very much about finances and had not expected to pay for our ourselves and had left the bulk of our money in our room. At the end of the evening we emptied our wallets and purses but found we didn't have enough money to hire a cab. We had no choice but to walk. I remember passing through Pigalle, where a beautifully made-up homosexual gave Sophie and me a look of hatred. After walking for over an hour we reached our hotel. We kissed our GIs goodnight and wished them luck. We were never to see or hear from them again.

As Sophie and I enjoyed the jazz club so much we decided to spend another evening there. We ordered a cab and paid our entrance fees and once again sat at a table near the bar. Sophie soon made friends with the bartender, who was another Italian living in Paris. She joked with the elderly manager, who was also behind the bar of the club. He was short and balding and well into his seventies. I didn't pay much attention to Sophie's conversations, preferring to watch the band and listen to the music. With the manager's permission the bartender began to supply us with rounds of free drinks. I smiled politely to them both and said, 'Thank you.' They smiled in return. Unbeknown to me the bartender asked Sophie if we could make up a foursome when the club closed. Sophie agreed and was quite happy for me to partner the elderly man. At closing time she told me to wait outside the club as we had a date. Soon the two men appeared. The bartender walked towards me and took my hand whilst the manager put his arm around Sophie. She stepped out of his embrace and made it clear that she wanted nothing to do with him. After a short discussion in French with the manager the bartender invited us to his penthouse flat with its view of the rooftops of Paris, just the three of us. We naively agreed.

It was a penthouse flat but comprised only a small double bedroom with a tiny bathroom and kitchen and a small roof garden. We went into the garden and saw the spectacular sight of the rooftops of

Paris in the early hours of the morning. We each drank a cup of coffee, all three of us sitting on the double bed as there were no chairs available. Soon the bartender took it in turns to kiss us. Sophie and I would do no more than that so an hour after we entered the flat our bartender telephoned for a cab and we returned to our hotel.

After breakfast we filled our suitcases for the long journey home. Sophie told me that every time she went on holiday she would get so excited she would menstruate unexpectedly. This had happened on this holiday and she had been forced to buy two packets of sanitary towels from a nearby pharmacy, but she only used the one packet. As she had bought souvenirs and presents her suitcase was overfull. She unwrapped the remaining sanitary towels and placed ten of them two deep at the top of her weekend case and locked it. Going through English customs Sophie was stopped by an official and asked to open the case. She blushed profusely and was extremely embarrassed. She looked at me and around her wondering what to do, saying, 'Oh no, oh no!' A small crowd gathered. I said to her, 'Sophie, give the man the key.' A red-faced Sophie did so. The official placed the case underneath the counter and unlocked it. He lifted the lid. Without changing his expression I could see him flicking through the layers of sanitary towels to see what was underneath them. He eventually closed the case, locked it and returned it to a mortified Sophie. We journeyed home without further mishap.

five
Ilfracombe, Devon
- 1966 -

S ophie invited me to a camping holiday in Ilfracombe, a seaside town in Devon, which she was
sharing with three of her other friends. She had
booked four nights at a campsite and a hired car to
take us there. I eventually met the other three girls,
Barbara, Dee and Clare. We were all in our early
twenties. Barbara was to drive the car as I had only
recently passed my driving test.

Sophie and I visited her sister, also called Sylvia,
and her husband John, to be shown how to erect
a large tent which they said we could borrow. We
wrote down their instructions and agreed it was
quite a simple task.

The five of us set off midmorning one Friday in
May in the hired car with Barbara at the wheel. We

motored down the major roads to Ilfracombe and arrived at the campsite, which we had found quite easily.

We tried to erect our tent in the space allotted but found we were unable to do so. Two ten-year-old boys saw our plight and came to our rescue. They told us they were boy scouts and had no difficulty in raising our tent from the ground into its upright position.

The campsite was quite large and sat on the top of the cliffs. There were many tents around us. The toilets and showers were housed in a building on the edge of the site and were reached by crossing the large field, which was extremely muddy due to the heavy rain that had fallen all day. There was a clubhouse containing a small supermarket and cafe. After we had showered and dressed we would dash there for a hot pot of tea and an English breakfast.

We spent our days travelling along coastal roads and the steep hills of Devon to other places of interest. We would walk down the cliffs to the beach warmly dressed due to the cold weather and bracing sea breezes. Of an evening we would have a drink in a pub.

On the last day of our stay Barbara drove to Ilfracombe's seafront, where we dined before our usual drink. At the end of the evening I drove back to the campsite. We were all desperate to pass water except Barbara. I drove her to our tent and then parked outside the toilets, finally returning to the tent. I took my foot off the accelerator ready to stop but the car picked up speed. I slammed the brakes on as we collided with the tent with Barbara inside it. She was completely untouched but lost her temper and swore at me saying 'You f— stupid cow! You could have killed me! That's a right bloody way to drive a car, isn't it!' She wouldn't listen to my explanation that there was a fault with the car and continued her tirade.

Being sworn at reduced me to tears. Barbara finally stopped yelling. Unfortunately the collision had uprooted one side of the tent. We used our suitcases to hold the canvas down and climbed into our sleeping bags. Then the wind began to blow. We saw flashes of lightning and heard the rumble of thunder. Soon we were in the middle of a thunderstorm.

After breakfast the following morning we packed our suitcases and dismantled the tent and started on the long journey home, with Barbara at the wheel.

Barbara overtook a car as we approached a railway tunnel. Too late she saw a deep puddle and had no choice but to go through it. A huge wall of water swept over the other car and muddy rainwater went straight through its open window. We looked round to see a young man in the driving seat with his wife and child beside him totally soaked. We gasped in horror as Barbara put her foot down. The driver gave chase and eventually caught up with us at a set of traffic lights. He stormed out of his car and spoke to Barbara. 'You completely drenched me and my wife and our baby. This is no way to behave, is it?' he asked.

We looked at his sodden jumper and wet hair and tried not to laugh. Barbara said, 'Sorry,' and drove off as the traffic lights changed. There were no further incidents and we reached London safely.

I have never been camping since that holiday.

six

Majorca, Spain
– 1967 –

Sophie and I had such an eventful trip the previous year we decided to journey abroad together again. This time we chose the island of Majorca, belonging to Spain. We booked a two-week package holiday departing the following August. On the due date we flew from Heathrow Airport. A coach and courier met us at Palma Airport, Majorca. There were approximately fifty people in our party. The coach stopped at various hotels dropping off guests. We arrived at ours shortly before lunch in the resort of Playa Arenal.

Our hotel was one of the best hotels I have stayed in. It was opposite a sandy beach and the blue Mediterranean Sea and had a large open-air swimming pool. A large bar and dining room were on the ground floor. The numerous waiters wore dinner jackets. Our room was twin-bedded with a bathroom and a small balcony.

I found Majorca to be a warm sunny island with a clear blue sea and friendly people. The majority of tourists were English and German. Building work had just begun on making a road around the island with the intention of producing more hotels and clubs to attract greater numbers of visitors.

After we had unpacked and freshened up we decided to take a stroll. A Spaniard walking towards us noticed our pale skins and said, 'Hello. Do you drink a lot of milk?' He was barefoot, wearing shorts and a T-shirt and was very deeply tanned.

Sophie and I managed to arrive downstairs for breakfast each day five minutes before the dining room closed at 11 a.m., due to the fact that we didn't go to bed much before 3 a.m.

We tried swimming in the sea but we didn't like the jellyfish that swam alongside us and the sand on the beach stuck to our suntan oil, so we chose to spend some hot afternoons lying by the hotel pool sipping iced cocktails served by waiters whilst we chatted to the other guests and slowly tanned our skins. We were soon in conversation with two girls from the north of England, Jackie and Irene.

They had been friends since their schooldays and had booked their holiday several months previously. Then Irene found a serious boyfriend but it was too late for her to cancel the trip. She missed him terribly and spent much of her time in tears and on the telephone to him in the UK. Jackie came out with us occasionally whilst Irene remained in the hotel room too upset to socialize wishing her holiday would end.

One afternoon Sophie and I travelled by bus into Palma. We walked around various historic buildings. As it was a hot afternoon we entered a cafe to quench our thirsts. Sophie ordered cold drinks at the counter. A very attractive blond Frenchman sitting there began to talk to her. She obviously liked him as she invited him to our table. He sat down and chatted to the two of us. When we left the cafe he followed us. To Sophie's dismay he took hold of my hand and spoke to me as we strolled up the road. We made a date for the three of us to meet on the beach the following day. After leaving the Frenchman Sophie complained that she would be the outsider so we did not keep our date.

Before our holiday Sophie had made me promise not to have single dates with men leaving the other person at a loose end and to only have foursomes.

I was quite happy to agree with this, which was why I didn't see the Frenchman. Unfortunately for me Sophie met a young German who asked her out and she made a date with him for the same evening. When I complained this was unfair and I would have nothing to do she told me I could sit in the hotel bar and talk to the other guests as we were friendly with quite a few people. I was very annoyed but she ignored my protests. She met her beau and returned to the hotel shortly after midnight. She told me she had spent the evening dancing but had made no further dates. I had spent my time in the bar as she had suggested.

Every evening Sophie and I went out after dinner, returning to the hotel at about 2 a.m. By this time there would be a group of married men seated at the bar whilst their wives slept upstairs. They always insisted on treating us to a drink. One evening we returned from a disco after having several drinks. The men bought us another two, then the barman suggested we should have a 'drink on the house'. We accepted. I watched him pour two large cocktails from a variety of bottles and noticed the colour change several times. I drank half the glass and soon I was extremely drunk. In the morning Sophie told me I had slapped a man around the face. I didn't remember that at all but I did remember his attempts to spray me with a soda siphon, which fortunately was empty. Four of the married men carried me to my room, leaving me leaning against the wall whilst Sophie unlocked the door and pushed me towards my bed. I managed to take my dress off and climb underneath the covers, falling asleep immediately. I woke the following morning without the slightest headache. It was the only time I have been drunk.

A few days into the holiday Sophie and I paid a visit to a local hairdresser to sort out our shoulder-length weather-beaten hair. The hairdresser successfully curled Sophie's into 'flick ups' and then attempted to style mine, which I usually wore piled on top of my head in curls. The result was acceptable but extremely Spanish. So much so that a Spaniard at a disco asked me to dance in his native tongue and then in English when he realized I hadn't understood him.

Sophie and I noticed the bottle of wine we had saved for lunch and dinner was emptying rapidly. We made a mark level with the wine before it was stored. The next mealtime we noticed the wine had gone down considerably. We loudly accused the two young waiters who served us. They told us to be quiet because we could get them into trouble. Not being unkind we said no more and watched our wine slowly disappear. Our waiters would joke with us, blowing us kisses and whispering in our ears, 'Me and you hot kisses under the table?'

As I was leaving the dining room one lunchtime the tall handsome head waiter approached me and asked if he and his brother could take me and Sophie out that evening. I accepted the invitation and a date was made for 9.30 p.m. at the bar of a neighbouring hotel as the waiters were not allowed to socialize with guests. His brother was also one of our waiters. He was short and fat and I found him to be very unattractive. We met at an appointed time. The short waiter put his arm round me while his brother held Sophie's hand. I had been under the impression that the tall waiter was my date for the evening. I refused to go out with his brother, who clung to my hand saying, 'Please, please.'

I said to Sophie, 'I'm going back to the hotel.' She laughed and followed me, leaving the brothers to spend their evening without us.

One evening the hotel hired a band to play in the bar area. Our head waiter gave the most awful rendition of the song 'Granada'. He was full of confidence and obviously considered himself a good singer as he sang at the top of his voice, unfortunately completely off-key. Several guests laughed behind their hands but politely clapped loudly when the song was over. Sophie and I wondered why his brother didn't tell him how badly he sang and the stifled laughter he created.

Sophie and I spent a few afternoons shopping for souvenirs and presents for those at home.

We booked two events through the courier. One was a nightclub with flamenco dancing in the cabaret, and the other a barbecue. The flamenco dancing was excellent and the entertainment was heightened when a juggling act dropped their skittles.

At the barbecue the dinner was free and we thought the drinks were as well. Two young Norwegian men asked if they could join our table. We agreed and they ordered a round of drinks. We chatted with them. All was well until a man from our party came up to the table and asked me to dance. I didn't like to offend him so I accepted. Sophie was asked to dance by a total stranger and she too accepted. When we returned to our table our Norwegians were very rude to us. They complained how bad mannered the English were and that we were a nation of ruffians, quoting an incident in their hotel when a group of Englishmen nearly drowned one of their friends in the pool and the man had to be resuscitated. They stood up and walked away from us. It was then we saw the dish with the bill and a banknote and we realized the drinks were obviously not free. At the end of the evening I picked up my handbag from under the table and discovered a large cigarette burn straight through the middle of it.

We spent the last evening of our holiday in the bar, chatting to the other guests who were now our friends, and exchanging addresses. We were both lightly tanned and sad that our holiday was over.

On the return journey the coach stopped at various hotels picking up holidaymakers. One Englishman boarded the coach as white as a sheet. We were told he'd spent the first day of the holiday sunbathing on the beach but had fallen asleep for some hours. A doctor diagnosed sunstroke and he had spent the entire fortnight ill in bed.

Seven

Betws-y-Coed, North Wales

– 1968 –

I shared an office with another secretary in a chartered accountants' in the City. She told me her younger sister Sandra had few friends and suggested we meet to socialize. This we did. We were all in our twenties. Sandra suggested we have a long weekend in Betws-y-Coed, as she had heard this was a picturesque village in North Wales.

We set off early one Friday morning in June in my black Hillman Imp car. We drove along the motorway to Birmingham and eventually through the mountains of Snowdonia. We reached Betws-y-Coed several hours later and booked three nights' bed and breakfast in a small family house. We discovered we were the family's only lodgers. There were no problems in having a bath every day but we would hang our wet towels over the wardrobe doors, which obviously annoyed our landlady as we would find them folded neatly over the back of a chair on our return.

We went sightseeing through the village and noticed that the locals were speaking in English. As soon as they saw us they would speak in Welsh. We entered a bakery to buy a sandwich. We were served in silence and were met with hostile stares from the other customers.

We walked along the footpaths and saw rolling hills and streams. We also travelled by car to explore the area. Unfortunately we lost our way. We asked an elderly gentleman standing at the front gate of his cottage for directions back to Betws-y-Coed. He totally ignored us. We eventually saw a signpost and were able to find the road returning us to our lodgings.

We drove to Caernarfon Castle and admired its beauty and shopped in the market immediately outside it.

Of an evening we would drink in a pub as there was no other form of entertainment.

On the last day of our stay we bade our landlady goodbye and placed our cases in the boot of the car. Unfortunately I was unable to start it. I asked her if she could recommend a garage. Instead her husband helped us. He lifted up the bonnet and repaired the fault.

We drove down the motorway in the fast lane at a speed of 70 m.p.h. Suddenly one of the tyres blew, which resulted in the car travelling from one lane to another whilst I tried to regain control. Sandra screamed at the top of her voice. I didn't blame her. Fortunately there were no cars alongside us. I looked in the rear mirror in the windscreen and saw several cars successfully dodging each other as I was forced into their lanes. Eventually I was able to pull over to the hard shoulder. A green Mini followed us. A bearded man stepped out and said, 'I'll change that tyre for you.' I was delighted and thanked him. Without his help we would have had a lengthy delay. Our Samaritan told us he was a professor at Birmingham University. We arrived home safely.

eight

Dunwood, Devon

– 1968 –

Anna and I met on a railway platform. We both caught the same train to the office every day and eventually began speaking to one another. We became friends and would occasionally socialize. As I had a car and Anna hadn't I used to collect her from the home she shared with her middle-aged parents, whom I soon knew as Rosemary and John, and I would return her at the end of the evening. Anna was a twenty-four-year-old divorcee. She was two years my senior and was tall and slim with shoulder-length natural blonde hair. We both smoked cigarettes.

Anna and her parents decided to take a week's holiday in the summer in a luxury caravan in Dunwood, Devon, and invited me along too. It was settled that we would travel there in my black Hillman Imp car. I also lived at home and the day before the holiday my father gave me £7 towards my 'spending money'. He also checked my car to see if I had enough oil and water for the journey, as well as tightening up any loose connections.

On the Saturday morning we set off to Dunwood. Approximately twenty miles from the resort a red light appeared on the dashboard. I could see that it was not the oil light so I decided to drive to the caravan park and sort out the problem the following morning. The next day I drove to a local garage to have my car repaired. A few hours later I returned and was told, 'Somebody has tightened up your fan belt and it's burnt out the dynamo. It's going to cost you seven pounds,' which was quite a lot of money and precisely what my father had given me. I realized he was responsible for the damage. I paid the bill and collected my car.

The caravan park was situated on top of the cliffs. A staircase led down to the beach and sea. There was a supermarket and a clubhouse with a bar on the site. Our caravan was large and slept four people comfortably. Rosemary and John very kindly allowed Anna and me to have the double bedroom whilst they slept in the lounge at the other end of the caravan, converting the settee into a double bed. The caravan also provided a large kitchen–diner and a small shower room with a toilet. I parked my car on the grass nearby.

Devon is a beautiful part of south-west England. Small towns are set amongst rolling green hills and valleys, edged by soft sandy beaches and the Atlantic Ocean.

Rosemary bought a week's supply of food from the park's supermarket and we sat down and sorted out the bills, splitting the petrol, food and the park's charges four ways.

Unfortunately we had a bad start to the holiday. Both Rosemary and Anna referred to John as 'big head'. I thought this was a friendly joke so I also began to call John 'big head'. Some time after my last comment John had reason to speak to me. He finished his sentence with a glare and snapped, 'OK, big head!' Too late I realized I was an outsider and should not have been so familiar.

Anna and I frequently walked down to the beach and spent our time swimming and sunbathing. Although her parents came with us occasionally and dipped their feet in the sea they preferred to sit outside the caravan during the day and spend their evenings in a nearby pub. Anna and I drove to a local beauty spot but only Rosemary joined us. John preferred to relax at the caravan site. The clubhouse was filled with children so Anna and I chose to spend our evenings further afield.

One day Rosemary served an excellent cold chicken salad with all the trimmings for our tea. She placed a large unopened jar of beetroot on the table. Anna picked it up but was unable to open it. John was seated at the table wearing only a white vest and trousers. She passed the jar to John for him to open. John picked up his fork and stabbed the lid of the beetroot jar and then gave it a huge tug, with the result that the lid came off with great force and the red juice splashed his face and saturated his vest. Beetroot juice dripped off him. I thought this was hysterically funny and burst into peals of laughter. Unfortunately no one else saw the funny side. John washed his face in the kitchen sink and turned his brightly spattered vest around the other way with the clean side facing the front. He had not brought another vest with him. Rosemary didn't wash it out so John wore the vest back to front for the remainder of the holiday, keeping his jacket on when he left the caravan.

One evening Anna and I drove into town and decided to have a drink in a pub. We met two young men who were locals and were soon in conversation with them. They very kindly bought our drinks. At closing time we gave them a lift to their homes but no dates were arranged. We simply kissed them and bade them goodnight. We arrived at the park at approximately 11.30 p.m. and promptly went to bed.

Rosemary had stayed in watching television whilst John had spent his evening in the local pub. He returned home around midnight and we gathered he was drunk. He slammed the main door and stumbled across the lounge. Soon Anna and I dissolved into giggles as the caravan and our double bed began to shudder. The shuddering continued for approximately ten minutes and we realized her parents were making love in the lounge. The incident was not referred to at all the following morning.

On the Friday evening Anna and I decided to drive to a nightclub in Exeter which we had seen advertised on the clubhouse notice board. Anna navigated and we had no trouble locating the nightclub. We sat down at a table immediately beside the dance floor and spent our time drinking, dancing and enjoying the cabaret. We laughed at the jokes of a comedian and listened to the voice of a woman singer. We did not find any boyfriends. Our problems began on the way home. I saw a 'no entry' sign positioned between two roads, one very narrow and one much wider. I chose to drive up the wider of the two but discovered my mistake when we approached a bend. We met six cars travelling towards us and successfully dodged them all but we were amused to see one of the drivers cross his eyes and pull a face as he drove round us. We eventually drove out of the street unscathed but realized we were totally lost. It was after 1 a.m. in the morning and we found ourselves in a residential area. Anna saw a young man walking ahead of us on the pavement and said, 'Give that feller a toot and I'll ask him how to get back to the main road.' In the stillness of the night my hooter sounded very loudly. The man was so shocked he jumped one foot in the air. We both giggled as I pulled over and Anna lowered her window. He gave us correct instructions to the main road and we arrived at the caravan without further mishap shortly after 2 a.m.

On the Saturday morning Anna and I hastily packed our suitcases. After a large breakfast cooked by Rosemary we began the long journey home, stopping at intervals for refreshments and reaching our homes in the early evening.

nine
Lloret de Mar, Spain
- 1974 -

Neil and I decided to have a second holiday together. We chose a two-week package in September in the resort of Lloret de Mar, Spain. At that time I became nervous of flying so, much to Neil's annoyance, I insisted we travelled by train, crossing the English Channel by the ferry. On our departure date various couriers made sure our party made all the right connections. We travelled through France and slept in couchettes overnight arriving in Spain mid-morning the following day. Unfortunately when the train stopped at our destination the driver did not allow sufficient time for his passengers to alight. Neil and another man were busy passing suitcases out the window to the waiting group on the platform when our train began to leave the station with four of us still on board. The men rapidly finalized their task. The courier called out, 'We've got all your suitcases so don't worry about them. Get off at the next stop and hire a cab to take you to the Buckingham Hotel in Lloret.'

Neil and I ran to the doorway as the train picked up speed. He said to me, 'Jump.'

I looked down at the platform as we sped along it and replied, 'No. I'll hurt myself.' So we remained on the train. Neil made no adverse comment. We returned to our seats, rejoining the other couple, and followed the courier's instructions, arriving at our hotel much later than expected.

The hotel was enormous, comprising eighty bed-rooms, a vast dining room and a large open-air swimming pool, overlooking the beach and Mediterranean Sea. Every Saturday night a band was hired and a dance was held in the dining room. This event was very well attended. Our room was on the second floor and was twin-bedded with a bathroom and a balcony.

Lloret at that time of year was very warm during the day and suitable for sunbathing but after 4 p.m. it became far too cold to lie on the beach. It was full of tourists, the majority of them English and German. It was very commercialized with plenty of shops, nightclubs and bars. We saw fish-and-chip shops catering for English tastes. A long main road hemmed with palm trees separated the beach from the town.

Neil and I would sunbathe either by the hotel pool or on the beach, occasionally swimming. I slowly tanned. Neil with his fair skin didn't. As the days passed by his skin changed colour from cream to pink slowly darkening until he became as red as a lobster. We spent most of our time in Lloret but we did travel by train to two other Spanish towns. We also journeyed around the Spanish coastline by boat. After dinner we usually walked along the front returning to our hotel room around 11 p.m. I noticed how tidy-minded Neil was. He would wash his shirt and underpants daily, hanging them over a chair on the balcony to dry.

As breakfast in the hotel was uninteresting we frequently ate an English breakfast in one of Lloret's many restaurants, only going to the dining room for early morning coffee. We had full board and shared our dining table with an English married couple called John and Denise. John was in his late forties and fifteen years older than his wife. It was his second marriage and her first. Initially we found them both to be very friendly and good fun. John would relate amusing tales from his days as a soldier in the British army based in Germany. Denise was very well endowed. When the food was slow in being served John would say to her, 'Whack one of your boobs on the table and we might get some service.' Then John advised Neil how to fight. He said, 'If you look like you're going to be the loser, stick your fingers up the other feller's nose and do your best to pull it off. That always works for me.' This comment disgusted Neil and me and we no longer enjoyed their company. Also the Spanish waiters serving our table seemed to be hostile towards us and at times we considered them to be swearing at us. The food was awful. We were served fish every second evening. John and Denise would complain loudly. After a few days they would only attend breakfast as they preferred to eat elsewhere. Around this time the electricity generator broke down and it was two days before it was repaired. This meant we had to bath in cold water, and lunch and dinner would be cold meat and salad, the latter eaten by candlelight. Fortunately for us John and Denise found this to be the last straw. They made strong complaints to the courier and arrangements were made for them to be compensated and flown home only six days after their arrival.

1974

On the seventh day of our holiday Neil told me he was constipated and had not defecated since arriving in Spain. I advised him to buy a bar of Ex-Lax from one of the local pharmacies. He agreed it was a good idea but insisted that I should be the one to ask for it. The first pharmacy we went into didn't sell it. The second one had run out but I was told to try a third pharmacy further along the road. Once again I asked, 'Could I buy a large bar of Ex-Lax, please?' This time I was successful.

As I paid the assistant Neil said in a very loud voice, 'Have you got what you wanted?'

Later that evening, and unbeknown to me, Neil chose to eat the entire bar of Ex-Lax. Fortunately I was the first to go to the toilet the following morning. Neil entered the bathroom as I left it, locking the door behind him. After some time had passed he returned to the bedroom. He said, 'I've just been to the loo at last and now the cistern won't work. You're not allowed in the bathroom until I fix it.' I lay on my bed giggling as I watched Neil stand on the toilet seat reaching up to repair the cistern. I realized the toilet must have been an unpleasant sight and laughed at the thought of what might happen if Neil couldn't get the cistern working. After some forty-five minutes had elapsed

Neil finally managed to flush the loo. I was then allowed in the bathroom to have my daily bath.

Whenever I passed reception without Neil beside me the two Spanish men behind the counter would wink at me and try to engage me in conversation. If Neil was with me they would act as though they hadn't seen me.

Walking around the back streets of Lloret we discovered many stray cats and noticed that English tourists were feeding them snacks bought from supermarkets. We wondered how the cats fared in winter.

Lloret had a large colourful market with many shops and stalls. We would wander around it buying presents and souvenirs. Neil bought himself the largest T-shirt sold on one of the stalls. He tried it on in the hotel room but he was unable to persuade it past his chest. We returned to the stall the following morning and Neil had his money refunded. We decided the Spaniards in that area must be rather short.

Relaxing on the beach one afternoon we watched the passengers disembark from a pleasure boat. We saw a middle-aged Englishwoman walk down the jetty wearing trousers and a bikini top. She must have raised her arms during the boat trip as the bikini top had risen, giving the appearance of a band around her chest, revealing the lower half of her breasts. We decided that she must have travelled by herself as obviously no one had told her of her disarray.

Apart from the Saturday night dances held in the hotel, Neil and I only spent one evening socializing with our party. We bought tickets for a flamenco show in a local nightclub. Our table was next to a party of eight Germans who sang Bavarian beer songs very loudly during breaks in the music. The flamenco dancing was excellent. We chatted to various members of our group and joined in the disco dancing. A local photographer snapped us seated at our table. We collected the photograph the next afternoon and were delighted to see it was excellent and worthy of framing.

Neil and I had a very relaxed holiday, getting plenty of sleep and fresh air. Despite the conditions at our hotel we were sad to leave Lloret. On the last day we rejoined our party for the journey home. I was fast asleep in my couchette on the train when Neil woke me in the middle of the night and told me to look out the window. I saw we were travelling at great speed over what appeared to be an enormous French lake. The water did not seem to be more than a yard below us and it was quite frightening. We soon returned to dry land and I eventually went back to sleep.

We were allowed two hours to shop in the duty free at the ferry terminal. A middle-aged man from our group had run out of French coins and almost begged me to give him one so that he could use the public toilet, saying, 'I'm absolutely desperate and I'm too scared to cough.' I gave him the requisite coin and later saw him on the ferry. He seemed to be relaxed and happy so I gathered he had solved his problem.

On our arrival in London we all shook hands and wished each other well, going our separate ways.

ten

Esbjerg, Denmark

– 1975 –

One evening Neil passed a travel agent and saw a weekend trip to Denmark advertised in the shop window at half its normal price. He entered the shop and asked for details. He showed me the brochure. I had not visited Denmark before. I agreed with Neil that it should be an interesting trip as we would journey there and back on board a Danish ship. Neil booked the holiday, departing one month later at the end of October.

On the due date we travelled to Southampton docks from London early in the morning in the coach provided. I gasped when I saw the ship. It was so high it looked to me like a floating block of flats. Our cabin was twin-bedded and without a porthole. The boat contained an enormous self-service restaurant and an equally large bar, run by smiling Danish seamen. There were various shops selling duty-free goods. Unfortunately the weather was bad and the sea was extremely rough. We sat in the big picture window of the bar facing forward. I watched in horror as the ship rolled deeply and back again as we ploughed through the giant waves below us. The only way to move across the boat was to run and grab the nearest pole or other object that was nailed to the floor, steady yourself and then run again.

A great many passengers were sick and vomit could be seen in corners and outside the toilets from those who had been unable to get there in time. We eventually went on deck, wrapped in winter clothing as the wind was fierce. Neil spent his time examining the many floors of the huge ship whilst I sat on a wooden chair looking out to sea and braving the elements. By bedtime I was feeling very unwell, caused by the constant swaying, and I thought I was going to vomit. As I didn't think I would sleep I swallowed a sleeping tablet and wondered what the result would be. The tablet had two effects. I drifted off to sleep and the sickness in my stomach abated.

We eventually docked in Esbjerg. A coach drove us to a large aquarium where various fish and seals were displayed. We bought our lunch in the restaurant within the complex. Then we boarded the coach and were driven to a small Danish village where we were treated to Danish pastries and tea in the local hotel. I visited the washroom and was surprised to see a circular bar of soap impaled on a long iron prong implanted in the basin, making it difficult for those inclined to steal the soap to do so. We were allotted forty minutes to walk around the village, which contained a few souvenir shops and a similar amount of houses. The coach returned us to the ship. I noticed lampposts moving to and fro in the wind as we sped along the Danish highways.

On the homeward journey the sea was still as stormy but this time it did not upset my stomach. I was woken from my sleep by Neil. He had not brought his watch with him and wanted to know the time. He switched on the small bedside lamp and put his right arm under my blankets searching for my left wrist, which he pulled towards him. We both discovered the time was 1.45 a.m.

On the coach to London, Neil explained that our cabin did not have a porthole because we were under the water level. He had thought it unwise to say so at the time.

I would not recommend a boat trip out of season.

eleven
Shanklin, Isle of Wight
- 1981 -

I met Judy at a social club. She was a secretary working for the Civil Service. She was dark haired, plump and two years my senior. We became friends. We would socialize by attending dances and walking through the parks on Sunday. She invited me to a long weekend in the town of Shanklin on the Isle of Wight, staying with her married friends who lived there. We decided we would travel there one Friday evening in mid-June. I left Judy to book the boat train from London to Portsmouth, where the ferry would take us to the island.

On the day of our departure I spent my lunch hour shopping in a supermarket close to the office, buying meat and groceries to cover our three-night stay, leaving the shopping in the refrigerator in the company's kitchen. Halfway through the afternoon Judy telephoned me. She was very upset as she found she had booked the train to Portsmouth but had not booked the ferry. She had tried to rectify the matter but was told by British Rail's clerk that our train would arrive at Portsmouth after the last ferry had sailed. Judy told me we either travelled to Portsmouth and stayed in a hotel overnight, catching the ferry the next morning, or we caught the boat train the following day forfeiting our original train fare as the clerk told her the money would not be refundable. We decided to travel to Portsmouth as planned.

We found ourselves a reasonably priced twin-bedded room in Portsmouth. After breakfast the next morning we set off for the island. I noticed a funny smell as I picked up the shopping bag and discovered that all the meat had gone bad overnight. I told Judy. We salvaged what we could of the groceries and left the rotting food in a paper bag in the waste bin in the hotel room. Judy paid me half the cost of the shopping.

We arrived at Shanklin mid-morning and hired a cab to take us to Judy's friends' home. They were both elderly. They made us very welcome. They lived in a large detached house in the centre of town.

I remember their furniture seemed to be very grand 1940s style and possibly worth a lot of money. They showed us to a flat in the attic that was to be our accommodation for the weekend. The couple owned a huge brown mongrel. I noticed all the carpets were covered in the animal's hair as clearly they did not vacuum very often. They were quite happy to allow us to use their home as a hotel. Judy and I spent our time taking healthy walks along the coastal roads, chatting to her friends at the end of our day. The weekend went without further mishap and we returned to London late that Monday afternoon.

twelve
Kirchbichl, Austria
– 1983 –

I met Elizabeth at a party held by a mutual friend. She was forty-two years old, a slim brunette spinster four years my senior. We began talking to each other as we poured wine into our glasses in our friend's kitchen. I had known her approximately half an hour when she told me she would like to go on a skiing holiday but had no one to go with. To my surprise she invited me. Despite realizing this to be a hasty decision, I agreed. Elizabeth told me she was employed by an agency as a temporary copy typist and had a long-term booking in the City. As she didn't earn much money and would not be paid for time off her holiday would have to be inexpensive. She gave me her address and we arranged that

I would call there with various winter sports brochures.

I drove to Elizabeth's home and she showed me into a small box room which she rented. She served coffee and we sifted through the brochures, finally choosing a ten-day mixed skiing and sightseeing holiday in the Tyrolean village of Kirchbichl in Austria, travelling there and back by coach in mid-March. Elizabeth wondered what clothing she should take and opened a wardrobe door to reveal a total of nine outfits, this being her entire supply of clothing. We decided that she would have to buy a ski suit that she could ill afford. I was fortunate enough to have a friend loan me hers. I booked the holiday the following morning.

We joined the other holidaymakers at Victoria Coach Station and boarded the coach, travelling first to Dover to catch the ferry. I noticed the toilet at the rear of the vehicle but at no time during the trip did I use it. We had a smooth crossing and made many purchases in the duty-free shop. The coach took us through Belgium and Germany into Austria throughout the day and overnight, stopping at various refreshment centres. I looked out the windows to see the now familiar scenery. Elizabeth pointed out that my right knee was over her space.

I promptly squeezed myself back to my side of the seats.

Kirchbichl was quite a large village containing many shops and houses. Our hotel was spacious and the centre of village life. It comprised a large bar, a huge dining room and a fair-sized indoor swimming pool. Our room was on the second floor. It was twin-bedded with a washbasin. The bathroom was further down the passageway and we shared it with several other guests. We were served breakfast and an evening meal and we both agreed the food was excellent. Unfortunately for Elizabeth our hotel room overlooked a cemetery and a church sporting a large clock which resounded every hour. Elizabeth was a light sleeper and the clock was to wake her every time it chimed throughout the night. Being a heavy sleeper I was not disturbed.

From the moment we boarded the coach Elizabeth seemed unable to talk about anything other than skiing. She continually told me how she was looking forward to the moment we would be on the slopes wearing our skis. She spoke of 'après ski' events with great excitement. The day after our arrival the coach drove our party to the ski centre where we paid £30 for the hire of skis and tuition for a week. Our instructor was an Austrian called

Karl who was tall and dark haired and I guessed to be in his late thirties. I quite fancied him but he didn't seem to notice me. Karl endeavoured to teach our group of eight British tourists how to ski on the lower slopes of the mountain. He succeeded with the other six.

I managed to balance on my skis as Karl showed the group the basic movements of skiing and how to stop by forming the shape of a snowplough. We took it in turns to ski down the mountain. Although I remained upright I was unable to stop. Karl would call after me, 'Where is your snowplough?' but to no avail. The only way I could come to a halt was to deliberately fall over. Elizabeth didn't fare much better. She spent the day doing her best to ski but she had difficulty in standing and frequently collapsed in a heap. She found skiing down the mountain to be very frightening and she too was unable to stop unless she fell over. As the coach returned us to the hotel in the early evening she told me she thought skiing to be too dangerous so she didn't intend trying any more. I was very surprised after her earlier excitement and the money she had spent on her suit. Despite the fact that I felt as though I was on an army manoeuvre I decided to continue with my skiing leaving Elizabeth to amuse herself during the day. She chose to walk around the village on her own. I found I mixed quite well with the others and would join them at a table when we had lunch in the ski-hut.

On my third day of tuition, instead of walking sideways up the mountain to rejoin the group, which is how you get up hill on skis and which made my legs ache, I decided to take the small electric rope lift up the lower slope. I positioned myself in a standing position as Karl had taught us, and with my left hand I grabbed the nearest of the two ropes to pull me up the mountain. I travelled quite successfully until an Englishwoman ahead of me fell over. As I would have collided with her because I was unable to stop I was forced to fall over too and found myself sitting in a twisted position in the snow with one leg underneath me and my neck wedged between the two moving ropes. A young ski instructor passed me. He saw my plight but instead of helping me he called out, 'Try to be more careful next time.' I managed to free myself but decided that skiing was far too hazardous and spent the remainder of the holiday swimming in the hotel pool (watched by Elizabeth who hadn't brought a swimsuit with her) and on excursions with the coach accompanied by Elizabeth. I noticed all the children were soon expert skiers, presumably because they had no sense of danger. At the end of the holiday Elizabeth and I were to return home still unable to ski.

Elizabeth was not properly dressed for the holiday. She had packed her ski suit and a pair of walking shoes but in the evening she wore the one summer skirt with a choice of two skimpy tops and high-heeled sandals. Apart from these items she had packed only one pair of jeans and two sweaters. I noticed she had brought a packet of three Durex with her. She told me this was in case she met a man she liked and he was not properly prepared. I was amused to see she had only one condom left in the packet.

I found our trip to be extremely cheap. Apart from a night-time visit to an ice rink, all the other evening entertainment and day trips were free of charge. The coach was also available for free use during the day. In the mornings it would take the skiers to the lower slopes of the mountains and around midday it travelled to Utters, returning to Kirchbichl late in the afternoon to pick up the skiers and return them to the hotel. I told Elizabeth about my first trip to Austria at the age of eighteen when I had stayed in Utters and had met the Austrian,

Rudi Meier. Throughout the holiday I had seen coaches pass us with his name painted on the side and had noticed ski centres bearing his name. I decided to travel to Utters with the coach to see if Rudi and his travel bureau were still there. Elizabeth agreed to come with me.

The coach approached Utters and drove down its main road, parking behind the hotel I had stayed in with Grace all those years ago. Elizabeth and I alighted.

I looked around me in astonishment. What had once been a tiny village was now a small town. The main street was full of smart shops with apartments above them and there were many houses in what had been the fields behind them. We walked to the travel bureau. Instead of a log cabin I now saw an elegant shop. Apart from the church the only building not to have altered was the hotel. Elizabeth and I entered the travel bureau. A young Austrian woman served me. I asked her, 'Is Rudi Meier here, please?'

Speaking in perfect English she replied, 'No, I am afraid not. He is in Innsbruck for the next few days. Did you particularly want to see him? I could contact him for you?'

I replied, 'No, thank you, but when you speak to

him would you tell him Sylvia of twenty years ago came in to see him.'

She replied, 'I will certainly do that. He will return in a few days' time.'

I thanked her and we left the shop. I was disappointed but I decided not to try to contact Rudi again and wondered if he would remember me. Judging by everything I had seen he must have made a fortune. We spent the remainder of the afternoon sightseeing in Utters and caught the coach back to Kirchbichl.

Unfortunately Elizabeth and I had not got on very well together, spending much of our time arguing. Somehow snow got into the workings of my watch and it stopped. At regular intervals I would ask Elizabeth the time. My last request prompted the reply, 'Have a look at the village clock.' During a coach trip I ran out of cigarettes and borrowed three from Elizabeth, promising to repay them when we returned to our hotel room where I had a supply. On our return I gave her three cigarettes.

She said, 'This isn't fair. I bought my cigarettes at the bar and had to pay the full price for them. You bought yours in the duty free which is a lot cheaper. So I think you should give me six cigarettes not three.'

Somewhat surprised I replied, 'I don't believe you. I've given you your three cigarettes back. I won't borrow any more but you won't get an extra three out of me.'

On the return journey Elizabeth and I were barely speaking to each other. As nightfall approached she found she didn't have a blanket to keep her warm overnight on the coach. I offered to share mine but she flatly refused. We parted at Victoria Coach Station and went our separate ways. Although I have occasionally seen her in a London street neither one of us speaks to the other.

thirteen

Puddyford, Devon

- 1987 -

I belonged to a large social club in London and decided to take advantage of the holiday advertised in its monthly magazine. The club was offering a one-week stay in Puddyford, Devon, in mid-July, for the sum of £89, this amount also covering travel there and back in the club's minibus. I phoned their offices and spoke to John the organizer. I discovered we would be a party of twelve to be housed in two separate cottages, one for the women and the other for the men. I asked the names of the other holiday-makers and found I knew no one other than John and his girlfriend, Sally.

On the appointed day I arrived at the clubhouse by minicab one hour early. Two other club members were there. They introduced themselves as Simon and Ginnie. We were all in our forties. We were soon in conversation. Simon said, 'I'm driving to Devon in my car. Why don't you two come with me. It'll be more comfortable than the minibus and we can meet everybody down there.' Ginnie and I agreed. We told John our change of plans and set off in Simon's brand-new Ford. I sat in the passenger seat whilst Ginnie had the back seat to herself. Once on the motorway Simon said, 'If either of you two ladies is desperate for the loo just tell me and I'll get you there as quickly as possible.' Our journey went without mishap. We found the three of us had the same sense of humour. We arrived in Puddyford ahead of the minibus.

The cottages were large and situated in a small close with a shop at its entrance. Our accommodation comprised a kitchen–diner with a bathroom behind it to the right of the street door and a large TV lounge on the other side of the hall. There were three bedrooms upstairs. Ginnie claimed the double bedroom for herself. Three other ladies, Mary, Joan and Diane, chose the large bedroom containing three single beds. I occupied the remaining bedroom containing a set of bunk beds. John told me another guest would be arriving midweek and would be sharing with me. The cottage was surrounded by a small garden with a lawn and borders of brightly coloured flowers. We soon discovered the building was not sound-proofed as you could quite clearly hear any noise in any part of it. Ginnie was not pleased with our accommodation, considering it to be rather shabby, and complained to John, who pointed out that the holiday was quite inexpensive. The men were housed in a similar cottage a few doors further down the close.

Puddyford was a small town sat upon the cliffs in the south-west of England. It had rolling hills with farmhouses nestling in valleys, and gave panoramic views of the coastline.

Ginnie and I unpacked our suitcases. We walked to the local shop to buy the necessary groceries, splitting the cost between us, and noted how expensive it was. It was now late afternoon. On the way back we met Simon. He suggested, 'Why don't we go for a drive?' We accepted his invitation.

Simon drove through the countryside. We saw 'patchwork' fields with sheep grazing on their grass and breathed in the fresh air. Soon Simon's sense of humour took over. He delighted in driving down the hills at top speed and braking severely as we rounded the bend, which made me squeal in horror.

The more I squealed the faster he would drive. Ginnie sat in the back seat completely unperturbed. We were to spend several days sightseeing in Simon's car.

In the evening we joined the party in the pub at the bottom of the steep hill below the Close. Ginnie and I returned to the cottage before the others. It was after dark and we were amazed at the blackness. There was only the occasional street light and we were surrounded by fields. We trod very carefully up the hill.

The following morning I woke around 7 a.m. I could hear people shouting downstairs. I donned my dressing gown and went to investigate.

I heard Diane say, 'This is a stupid way to carry on.'

Ginnie replied, 'Well, I can be inconsiderate too.'

I realized the TV was blaring. I asked Ginnie, 'What's going on?'

Diane replied, 'She turned the TV on full blast this morning at 6 a.m. and woke the three of us up and she still won't turn it down.'

Ginnie replied, 'Well, you didn't mind waking me up at one o'clock in the morning when you three finally came back laughing and joking up the stairs at the top of your voices and slamming the street door, so you can put up with my noise now.'

Diane said, 'We're supposed to be on holiday and we're entitled to come home at one in the morning.'

Ginnie replied, 'Well, I think you should consider other people and I'm not going to stand for it.'

Someone eventually turned the TV down, which was immediately underneath the three women's bedroom. Later in the day Diane complained to John, who told Ginnie it was a childish way to behave, but this did not deter Ginnie. She woke early each morning and turned the TV set on full blast every day of the holiday. Diane chose to ignore Ginnie's behaviour.

Joan commented, 'I'm not getting involved in this.'

Mary said, 'Neither am I.'

I thought to myself: 'You're all in the same bedroom and the three of you upset her, plus she's waking you up too, so you are involved.' The blaring TV did not wake me. Although there was friction in the cottage I remained on friendly terms with everyone. But there was an icy silence between Ginnie and the three women.

The weather was typical of an English summer.

There was plenty of rain but some sunshine and it was quite warm.

There was much hilarity amongst the group. The average age was forty and we were all ready to have some fun. The men would visit our cottage during the day for cups of coffee and would sometimes appear with a bottle of alcohol of an evening.

Soon the last member of our party arrived. Her name was Helen and she was employed as a police-woman. Her choice of profession caused her a lot of teasing but she was on holiday and soon became just another member of the group. She shared my bedroom and slept in the lower bunk as I preferred the top. She told me she was trained to use a gun and occasionally climbed over walls whilst chasing criminals. She also told me she had a mortgage on a maisonette in London, that she ran a car and spent most of her free time on foreign holidays. As she wore her policewoman's skirt and shoes every day I decided she must spend her money wisely.

One evening we had a party in our lounge. As time passed I became very tired and went to bed. A few minutes later Simon crept into my room wearing only his underpants. I thought this to be hysterically funny. I said to him, 'Simon, you're wasting your time. Please go away.' He did so, donning the trousers he had left outside my bedroom door. In the middle of the night I must have stirred in my sleep as the blanket covering me slipped to the floor. This sensation caused me to wake with a jump and I yelled out.

My shout woke Helen, who asked, 'Are you all right, Sylvia?'

I replied, 'Yes, sorry,' and climbed down the ladder to retrieve the blanket. In the morning I discovered I had woken everyone in the cottage. Someone told Simon.

He said to me, 'I make a pass at you and you wake up screaming in the middle of the night.' He didn't believe my explanation and he didn't make another pass at me either.

Soon Simon's interest turned to Helen. She joined the three of us on a trip to a fishing village. As I approached his car Simon opened the rear door, smiled at me and ushered me into the back seat beside Ginnie. He then opened the front passenger door enabling Helen to sit beside him.

A few of us decided to walk through the countryside. As we were crossing a stream my right foot slid down the bank into the water and sank into thick mud, much to everyone's delight. When I managed to extricate myself I used clumps of grass to cleanse my foot and sandal.

One day Ginnie and I joined a party of five on a walk down to the harbour to watch the fishing boats. Soon the group decided to walk over the cliffs.

I said to them, 'Heights make me dizzy so I'll stay around the harbour and I'll see you lot at dinner.'

Their response was, 'Don't be silly. You'll be all right. We won't go near the edge and you can walk over the grass.'

Foolishly reassured I joined them. We climbed the hill to the top of the cliffs and I soon found we were forced to walk along the path as the grass was covered in bushes. I reluctantly continued and found myself looking down sheer drops of fifty feet which unnerved me. I said to them, 'I can't go any further. It's sheer drops everywhere.'

One of the men volunteered, 'Put your hands on my shoulders, don't look down and stay behind me,' which I did. This caused great amusement and Ginnie took a photograph 'for the club magazine'.

My worst moment came when I climbed over a stile unaided. I lifted my left leg high and looked down to see a sheer drop of almost seventy feet. I clambered over the stile and grabbed my helper's shoulders. Further along the path we met John and Sally, who were walking towards us. Everyone stopped for a chat. I moved as far from the edge as possible and sat down, wondering, 'How can you hold a conversation when you are standing two feet away from the edge of a cliff and certain death if you slip?' The conversation ended and we resumed our walk. I was very relieved when we eventually returned to ground level.

In the evening Diane was seated opposite Ginnie and me at the dinner table. Ginnie made a sarcastic remark directed at Diane. This time Diane broke her silence and answered in the same tone. Ginnie appeared very flustered and her face became bright red. They continued to exchange sarcastic comments until Ginnie said, 'Mutton dressed as lamb.' Diane did not reply further. It was some minutes before Ginnie regained her composure.

We all found time to do some shopping. I remember I bought pink spotted bath towels in a sale and a set of hanging chimes from a souvenir shop. Ginnie and I had a few words with the young shop assistant as she didn't want to open the box to show me the chimes were in working order.

On the last day of the holiday, Bill, a member of our party, knocked on our street door and asked if he could use our bathroom as there was a long queue for his in the men's cottage. As all the women were ready for the day we agreed. Unfortunately the bathroom door did not lock. Soon Simon entered the cottage and heard that Bill was in the bath. He grabbed my hand and dragged me down the hall to the bathroom. He opened the door wide and pushed me inside, closing the door quickly and holding on tightly to the doorknob so that I was unable to get out. By this time Bill was out of the bath. I noticed he flinched as I came into the room and then he stood still. I think he realized the folded bath towel over his left arm completely covered his private parts. He remained in that position until Simon finally released his hold on the doorknob several minutes later.

At 11.30 a.m. we made our way home. Once again I travelled with Simon in his car. He chose to take Helen and one of the men, leaving a very annoyed Ginnie to travel to London in the minibus. Once again Helen sat in the front passenger seat. We had a pleasant journey, occasionally stopping for refreshments. I arrived home around 9 p.m.

fourteen

Dartmouth, Nova Scotia

- 1987 -

Lorraine was Neil's sister. She was an attractive blonde six years my junior. Unfortunately Neil died in 1979 after a long illness but I remained friendly with his family. Their father was a Canadian soldier who had met and married their English mother whilst he had been based in London during the Second World War. They chose to settle in London. At the age of nineteen Lorraine emigrated to Canada and became close to that side of the family. She eventually ran a second-hand clothing business with her Uncle Harry. She would visit her parents frequently. On her last trip to London she asked me if I'd like to spend two weeks with her in Canada. I accepted her invitation with great excitement. The company I worked for allowed me to take time off. I booked my flight in early September to Halifax Airport, Nova Scotia, Canada, arriving one week after Lorraine had returned.

On the due date I travelled by tube to Heathrow Airport, allowing plenty of time to catch a midday plane. I checked in at the Air Canada desk. The clerk returned my passport to me saying, 'Would you please sign it.' I did so. We began chatting.

She asked me, 'Is this your first flight?'

I replied, 'No, but I haven't been on a plane for about twenty years and I'm a little nervous. Can you tell me where I go after I leave you because I've always travelled with package tours and never on my own before.'

She asked, 'Would you like someone to see you to the plane?'

I replied, 'Yes, please, that would be lovely.'

She said, 'If you wait at the blue kiosk opposite this desk, at eleven o'clock a stewardess will collect you and all you have to do is follow her.'

I replied, 'Thank you.'

I found a cafe and ordered a cup of tea. At a quarter to eleven I stood at the blue kiosk. Three people were waiting there. One was a fourteen-year-old girl who was travelling by herself to join her mother and new stepfather in Canada, an elderly lady seated in a wheelchair and a Spaniard who could speak no English. And then there was me. At the appointed time a stewardess arrived. She led us to the top of every queue and finally through the departure lounge and onto the bus that drove across the airport to the plane.

My seat was in the smoking section beside a window. The seat beside me was empty. I decided to watch take-off but regretted it a few minutes later. As the plane left the runway the houses I had been looking at appeared to be lopsided. I looked ahead of me and found the plane to be almost vertical. My stomach seemed to hit my chin. Without making a sound I closed my eyes and held my head until we finally stopped climbing. A voice over the intercom announced that we had reached 35,000 feet. Once my stomach settled down I relaxed and enjoyed the flight. I spent most of the journey looking out the window and could see the clouds and Atlantic Ocean beneath us. I tried watching the film and was amused to see it was entitled *The Black Widow*. An elderly Canadian couple returning to their home after a holiday in London took it in turns to sit beside me and smoke a cigarette as they were seated in the non-smoking area of the plane. It was a smooth flight but I was relieved when I eventually heard the 'thud thud' of landing on the runway.

As I cleared customs I looked for Lorraine but she was nowhere in sight. I bought refreshments in one of the cafes and asked the waitress how to use the telephone. Using the coins she gave me in my change I dialled Lorraine's number. I replaced the receiver as I realized I was hearing an unobtainable signal. I knew Lorraine's address and could have hired a cab to take me there but I chose to wait in the airport lounge believing there was some minor reason to explain her absence. Some two hours later I saw her hurrying across the airport towards me accompanied by an elderly gentleman she introduced as Uncle Harry. She told me that they had thought I was arriving on a later flight. Harry placed my luggage in the car he had parked outside the main doors and drove us along wide roads edged with fir trees to Lorraine's trailer home in Dartmouth.

The trailer was one of many in a large park. It was two-bedroomed with a small garden. The outside appeared to be made of heavy metal. Wire mesh covered the doors and windows to ensure it was insect-free. Inside was a very comfortable home. There was a large open-plan area containing the kitchen, lounge and dining room. A corridor led to a modern bathroom and two bedrooms, one of which Lorraine used as a sewing room. My bed was a convertible settee in the lounge. Zoe, Lorraine's sandy-haired mongrel, greeted me with a wagging tail.

Harry left the trailer shortly after we arrived. I was very tired after the journey. I was disappointed when Lorraine told me she had made arrangements for us to go to a disco with a woman called Irene who worked in her second-hand clothing shop. Lorraine told me I could stay in the trailer if I wanted to but the door would have to be left unlocked until her return. I didn't think I would sleep in an unlocked trailer so very reluctantly I decided to go to the disco. We left at 10 p.m. Canadian time. The time difference between Nova Scotia and the UK is four hours. This meant that I went out at 2 a.m. British time. We returned to the trailer five hours later. Because of this excursion I experienced jet lag. It was very unpleasant. I felt tired every second of the day for about a week.

Dartmouth is adjacent to Halifax. They are two small towns set deep in the Canadian countryside. Outside town vast roads seemed to have been cut through the dense fir trees. My first reaction to Nova

Scotia was wide-eyed amazement as I looked around me. Everything was so different. Most of the houses were made of wood. Both towns seemed alive with plenty of entertainment in the evenings. There were many bars and a great many country and western dances. The dances were great fun as the men asked the women to dance and we were never short of partners, which is more than I can say for London dances. I felt as though I was on a holiday of a lifetime. Lorraine took me sightseeing in her car. Tears trickled down my throat. When I could trust my voice to remain steady I said to her, 'Thank you for my holiday.'

She replied, 'Don't thank me. You're the one that's paying for it. I'm glad to have the company.'

My trip was inexpensive. I paid the return air fare which cost just over £300. There were no hotel bills or car hire. I paid my share of the electricity and went half on the petrol and food we ate in the trailer.

At one country and western evening a Canadian called Jim asked me to dance. He was in his thirties and was huge, wearing a thick black beard. When he discovered I was English he laughed and said, 'Does the Queen know you're here? Would she approve of you dancing with me? Can I take you for a cup of tea?' I did my best to respond to the fun by asking if he was a lumberjack. As he didn't reply I asked if he was living on benefit. We continued dancing. The band started to play a slow number. Jim pulled me closer to him. His open mouth moved across my cheek towards my left ear. Unfortunately I was wearing gold-plated long hoop earrings and one clinked against his teeth and entered his mouth. Undeterred he kissed my hair. His lips brushed against mine but he didn't kiss me. We danced together for what seemed like thirty minutes. Finally he said, 'I'm a ship's engineer. I'm sorry but tomorrow we sail for New Brunswick and I won't be back for three weeks.' I stayed with Jim until the end of the evening. We kissed goodbye but we did not exchange addresses.

As Lorraine and I entered the car park she saw a man she thought was a Red Indian. She walked up to him and asked, 'Are you a Red Indian?'

He replied, 'Yes.'

She continued, 'Would you shake hands with my friend as she's just come over from London and she's never seen a Red Indian before?' I was slightly embarrassed but shook the man's hand.

Harry was a frequent visitor to the trailer. He was a widower living on his own. His two adult children were married. I did not meet them. As I was on holiday he allowed Lorraine to take time off instead of helping with their second-hand clothing business. On the first Sunday of my stay he drove Lorraine and me a great distance along the coast to an area known as Peggy's Cove where a meteorite had landed years before, breaking into many rock formations. Unfortunately Harry's driving was awful. I would be seated in the back of the car while Lorraine sat in the front beside him. They would chat as we travelled. Harry was hard of hearing and would frequently lean over to Lorraine to hear what she had said, completely taking his eyes off the road. At times like these I would watch the road ahead and would yell 'Look out!' each time we neared a verge. I would have a sick feeling in my stomach. To my horror he overtook on a hill. A car came from the opposite direction. After much blaring of horns Harry squeezed in between the two cars he had attempted to overtake. Back at the trailer I told Lorraine I couldn't bear Harry's driving. She decided to tell him I was a nervous passenger and would he drive more slowly, which he did. This greatly improved my nerves on future trips. He was very polite and friendly towards me.

Every morning Lorraine would take Zoe, her

mongrel, for a walk around the trailer park. As dogs had bitten me as a child I am nervous of animals and I kept my distance from Zoe. On an evening spent watching Canadian TV and its many stations, Zoe walked across the lounge to the settee I was seated on. I had my hands crossed over my knees. Zoe sat beside me. She slowly eased her wet nose and muzzle underneath my right hand. Lorraine and I decided that was a clear indication that she wanted me to pet her. Zoe and I became great friends from that moment.

The Canadian people were very friendly towards me. I noticed how casually they dressed. Everyone seemed to wear only blue jeans and T-shirts. If I wore a dress or skirt or high-heeled sandals they all realized I was a foreigner. On hearing my English accent all heads would turn in my direction. This embarrassed me so I tried not to speak unless I had to. I mentioned this to Lorraine who advised, 'Forget all about it and leave them to stare.'

At a disco one evening I shouted over the music to the waitress at the snack bar, 'Could I have an egg roll, please?'

She shouted back, 'Sure,' adding, 'I just love the accent.'

I was occasionally asked directions. Everybody

believed me when I replied, 'I have absolutely no idea.'

I had already met Lorraine's Uncle Haddie when he had visited her parents in London the previous year. Harry told him I was in Dartmouth and I received an invitation to stay a few days in Haddie's home in the small town of Centerville, deep in the heart of the Canadian countryside. Harry drove me there with Lorraine sitting beside him. His driving was much slower but it was a great relief to reach Centerville. I met Haddie's wife Pat and her elderly widowed mother, Edna, who shared their home. The house was huge. It was made of wood, painted white and contained sixteen rooms. A vast lawn surrounded it. I was given a comfortable bedroom overlooking the back garden. Each day I was left to sleep until I woke naturally. Haddie was a retired TV sound technician. Pat was a few years younger than him and was employed as a schoolteacher. There was a no-smoking rule in the house as Pat was allergic to nicotine. Each morning when I woke up I would wrap a blanket around my nightgown and smoke my first cigarette of the day on the big wooden porch outside the street door. One morning I noticed the school bus drive past. A small boy spotted me. He must have found me very interesting as his eyes did not leave me until the bus was out of sight.

Haddie took me sightseeing each day, showing me the countryside and the occasional small town. At night I looked at a sky filled with stars. One day Haddie drove me along a coastal road and pointed to the bay below. He said, 'That's the Bay of Fundy. Make sure you always remember you have been here as it's a famous nature reserve.' One afternoon we collected Pat after her classes. We entered the schoolroom. I noticed computers at each child's desk. Pat told me she was teaching the children to speak Micmac, the language of a local Red Indian tribe. At my request Haddie returned me to Dartmouth, telling Harry he had some errands to run there.

Lorraine and I booked a Greyhound bus to take us on a three-day trip to Bangor in the state of Maine in the US. We arranged that Harry would collect us at 6 a.m. to take us to the bus station in time to catch the six thirty bus. Unfortunately on the day of our departure both Lorraine and I overslept. We were woken by the sound of Harry banging on the trailer door shouting, 'You guys have done it this time!' Lorraine let him in. We dressed at great speed whilst Harry made coffee. Fortunately we had packed our suitcases the previous evening. Harry said, 'I'll drive you to the next stop, at the airport, so we should get there ahead of the bus.' We finally set off in Harry's car.

Eight minutes into the journey Lorraine said, 'I've forgotten my passport!' I was not very pleased but Harry laughed. He turned the car round and we returned to the trailer where Lorraine quickly collected it. Harry drove as fast as he could through the traffic and we reached the airport a few minutes before the bus arrived. We eventually climbed aboard and chose two seats at the back of the vehicle. As we travelled along the highways Lorraine became very unwell. By the time we arrived in Bangor she was convinced she had a serious illness. She wouldn't listen to my claims that it was only travel sickness and returned to Canada at 1 a.m. on another Greyhound bus three hours after we had booked into a motel, saying 'I can't afford to be ill here. I haven't got my insurance.' I decided to stay and have my first glimpse of the US.

Bangor was a small town surrounded by countryside. The motel was situated beside a small airport. We had arrived at night time and I had noticed the gaudy lights of the restaurants and bars. Left to my own devices I asked reception each day, 'Where is there somewhere interesting to go?' As they only recommended shopping malls and parks, I chose to walk through the quiet residential streets filled with large wooden houses into the centre of town, where I bought souvenirs such as tea towels made in the US. In town the roads were wide and busy. I had a problem crossing them. When one lane of traffic stopped at the lights I would run across the road as quickly as possible before another lane of traffic would drive towards me. The first evening I set out to see Bangor at night but found the buildings were surrounded by countryside and darkness. As I considered myself unsafe alone, after dinner in a nearby restaurant I would return to my room to watch US TV. I caught the Greyhound bus in the early hours of the fourth morning and returned to Halifax, sleeping for most of the journey.

As soon as we reached the airport I left the bus and phoned the shop. Harry answered. I suggested I catch a cab to the trailer but he insisted that he and Lorraine would collect me. Half an hour passed. I phoned the shop again, this time speaking to Irene. She said, 'They've phoned in to say they can't find you anywhere.'

I replied, 'I'm sitting in the lounge area.'

Another half an hour passed. I phoned the shop again.

Irene said, 'They want you to stand by the swing doors.' I walked to the main doors of the airport.

Time passed again without the arrival of Harry and Lorraine. I phoned the shop again, speaking to Irene. I said, 'Tell them I'll catch a cab.'

She replied, 'OK, but they said they can't find you anywhere at the bus station.'

I replied, 'I'm not at the bus station, I'm up at the airport!'

Irene sighed and ordered, 'Sit down in the lounge and I'll send them there the next time they phone in.'

Twenty minutes later Harry and Lorraine walked through the glass doors towards me. Harry asked me, 'Why did you get off at the airport?'

I replied, 'Because that was where I got on the bus?'

Soon my holiday came to an end. After I had landed in Halifax I was told there had been quite a few 'near-misses' with aircraft in the area. This worried me. I chose to forget about it during my stay but I was soon to board my second flight in twenty years and my first night flight. I became very nervous. Harry, Lorraine and I travelled in the car to the airport. They stayed with me until I entered the departure lounge. We kissed each other good-bye. Eventually I took my seat on the plane, once again beside a window but this time overlooking the left wing with its revolving light underneath it. A tall man in his mid-thirties sat beside me. He smiled and we exchanged names. He soon engaged me in conversation. I noticed he wore a thick wedding ring on his left hand. We spent the entire night talking.

I jumped at the sound of a hissing noise. Carl said, 'That was only the air-conditioning.' I told him about the 'near-misses'. He replied, 'That may be so but the planes were all about five miles apart. If something goes wrong with this plane, land is only forty-five minutes away. You should relax and enjoy the flight.' He paused, then asked, 'What do you do for a living?'

I replied, 'I'm a secretary. What do you do?'

I was stunned when he replied, 'I'm an Air Canada pilot. I'm on my way to Germany where I start work flying planes.' I was immensely reassured. I felt like a sick patient sitting beside the doctor and I forgot my fears. We landed safely at Heathrow Airport.

Carl stayed with me until I collected my bulging suitcase. He said, 'Let me help you home with this.'

I replied, 'Well, I can't think what I'll do with you when I get there.' There was a heavy silence. I said, 'I'll be perfectly all right but I think I'd better call a cab rather than go by tube.' He walked away from me.

A few months later I received a very sad letter from Lorraine. She wrote that Harry had had an accident in his car in dense fog. He did not see or hear the truck travelling towards him that hit him as he made a 'U' turn in the fog on the vast highway. The emergency services cut him out of his car and he was rushed to hospital, where he died a few hours later.

fifteen

Turkey

- 1988 -

This particular year I had no friends available to go on holiday with and it seemed to me I would not be travelling anywhere. A colleague suggested I contacted a singles holiday club she had used the previous summer. I phoned their offices and asked for their brochure showing the variety of trips on offer. I leafed through the pages and finally chose a one-week package holiday in a large villa with its own swimming pool just outside Bodrum in Turkey for the following July. This was to be my first holiday on my own.

On the due date I travelled by tube to Heathrow Airport early in the morning to catch an 8.30 a.m. flight. Whilst waiting in the departure lounge I noticed another suitcase with the club's ticket attached to it and walked over to the man standing beside it. I introduced myself and he told me his name was John. We were quite obviously the first of our group to arrive. Slowly other members joined us, identifying us by the tickets on our cases, and we were soon a party of fifteen people aged thirty and upwards. Apart from one middle-aged married couple we were all total strangers. There was no courier at Heathrow to meet us so we found our own flight. We were not seated together on the plane but were some distance from each other. I decided the club must have booked plane seats as their customers purchased their holidays.

The flight was smooth and, as usual, I spent my time looking out the window as we flew over the countries beneath us. We landed at Dalaman Airport in Turkey some hours later, where we were met by the club's courier. Before boarding the waiting coach I visited the ladies' toilet. I entered the cubicle to see an open hole in the ground with concrete tiles around it. I chose to wait until we were at the villa where I hoped I would find a 'European' toilet, and returned to the coach. By this time flights from other parts of the UK had landed and our numbers swelled to thirty-four, the majority of us meeting each other for the first time. We boarded the coach and were driven through the mountains to the villa. The weather was very hot.

Peter, the villa's young Australian manager, sorted out who was sharing each room and gave out the room keys. I was partnered with a thirty-five-year-old schoolteacher called Jan. We shared a twin-bedded room with a shower on the ground floor. I was quick to tell her that although I was a smoker I realized if I smoked cigarettes in the bedroom this would make her clothes smell so I would smoke elsewhere. We soon became very good friends.

The villa was newly built and owned by a Turkish family who lived on the first floor away from the holidaymakers. It contained approximately twenty twin-bedded rooms each with a separate shower, all built around a small swimming pool with a bar to one side of it. The roof was flat and was reserved for nude sunbathing. The women were allowed to lie topless around the pool. The dining room was a large terrace on the first floor with a canopy over-head. Four young English women cooked our food. There were all cordon-bleu cooks and I was to look forward to meal times. Turkish maids, speaking no English, made our beds and cleaned our rooms each morning. Our shower room was the size of a bathroom and included a washbasin and toilet.

Unfortunately there was no type of guttering around the shower so soapy water would flood the entire floor until a small drain emptied it. Peter told us not to put toilet paper down the toilet. Instead we were to place it inside the bin provided, otherwise the sewage pipes would become blocked.

We had arrived at the villa around 2 p.m. After I unpacked I decided to change into my blue bikini and sunbathe and swim in the pool. Jan joined me, also wearing a bikini. Slowly everyone else appeared. Jan and I were the only women fully covered, all the others were topless. I was surprised to see that several well-endowed women I had noticed on the coach looked far better with their clothes on. One blonde woman, aged about thirty, looked terrific dressed in a T-shirt with a bra underneath but without them she displayed a completely flat chest with two breasts as big as watermelons hanging almost to her waist with her nipples facing the ground. We were surrounded by boobs of all shapes and sizes. Two sixty-year-old women wearing swimsuits had lowered their tops to expose enormous sagging bosoms. Also the ladies did not seem to worry about any excess pubic hair. Several of them had tufts of hair poking out around the bikini line. One young woman showed off pubic hair which formed a line all the way up to her navel. As the week progressed Jan eventually went topless. I didn't. One of the men asked me when I was going to. I replied, 'I'm sorry, but I'm a bit backward in that direction.'

Several club members became couples and began instant affairs, which resulted in the changing of bedrooms.

Dinner was at 9 p.m. and everyone dressed up for it. The food was excellent and equal to what you would expect to find in an expensive restaurant. But it seemed to me that the desserts, although delicious, contained at least 3,000 calories. As I didn't want to put on weight I just ate the first two courses and had a glass of wine, finishing the meal with a coffee. I was seated opposite Jan and beside Richard, a forty-year-old homosexual who was English but based in Geneva. I got on well with Richard and genuinely liked him. Other members of the group were extremely unkind to him, sometimes making him a figure of ridicule.

After dinner everyone stood at the bar drinking and talking. Unfortunately I don't like talking to groups of people. I did make the effort to socialize but I can be quite shy and I frequently found myself standing alone, talking to no one. So after dinner I would have one drink at the bar and if I didn't find anyone to talk to I would retire to bed. Other members would continue their entertainment by visiting discos, returning to the villa in the early hours and skylarking in the pool. This upset other club members who were sleeping and Peter would voice their complaints at dinnertime. Being a heavy sleeper they didn't disturb me.

The villa was one of many private villas along the coast and was set in semi-countryside. One hundred yards away there was a large German holiday camp from which booming Bavarian music could be heard late at night. Every day was extremely hot and sunny. I applied Factor 15 sun oil every hour and managed to tan without burning. I found the Turkish people to be polite and friendly.

I bumped into John as I came out of my room. I noticed he was wearing a wooden beaded necklace.

'How are you?' I asked.

'Fine,' he replied, adding, 'I've decided to stay another week so I'm cutting down on my dirty washing and I've given up wearing underpants.'

I replied, 'Oh, right. See you later.' I tried not to think of the condition of his shorts and trousers. As I passed the swimming pool Elaine, an older member of the group, called out to me: 'Do you fancy shopping in Bodrum with me today?'

'That's a good idea,' I replied.

We waited for the bus to take us there and spent the afternoon in Bodrum's colourful market. I discovered we were expected to haggle with the stallholders so I managed to buy many bargains, leatherware in particular was very cheap. One stallholder, speaking in perfect English, told me it was only in the tourist season he had work and that he had to save to support himself through the winter.

A few days into the holiday Richard complained to Peter that his washing was disappearing from the clothes line at the side of the villa. Peter warned everyone at dinner and as Richard was rather plump he raised a laugh when he added, 'So if you see a fat Turk wearing a green T-shirt, please inform me.'

Another day Richard told me he'd made friends with the local supermarket owner and his male assistants and invited me to a card party he was going to above the shop. As I had visions of a gangbang I politely turned down his offer. Richard also went shopping and was the cause of unkind laughter when he carried a manly handbag to dinner.

I realized I had an admirer. One of the men took

at least ten photographs of me in his own camera and one night at dinner he told me I looked 'absolutely smashing'. He was always engaging me in conversation. I overheard him say he had a girlfriend in the UK so I assumed this was why he didn't try to date me. He also participated in nude sunbathing on the roof of the villa.

Jan became very friendly with a man called Paul, who was a few years younger than her, but she too had a partner at home. She told me, 'I really like Paul. If it wasn't for my boyfriend in London I'd sleep with him.' Jan and Paul spent their days together and I would occasionally join them.

A group of us dined in a Turkish restaurant along the coast. Richard and my admirer came along. Halfway through the evening a curvaceous belly dancer appeared wearing a yashmak. She danced for several minutes on the dance floor and then on top of the tables. Appreciative men threw money in her path. When she danced on our table Richard held up a carefully folded banknote. She bent down and Richard gently patted the note deep into her cleavage until it disappeared, without touching her skin with his fingers. He also raised a few cheers when he stood up and mimicked her dancing.

Jan, Paul and I joined a small group of club

members on a day trip to Bodrum and its castle. We boarded a bus to take us there and walked along Bodrum's waterfront, passing the many boats moored there, some of which offered trips around the coast. We also passed some very smelly camels the tourists could ride for a few coins. We climbed the battlements of the castle and admired the wondrous views out to sea. Afterwards we walked through the back streets of Bodrum and looked through the railings of a mosque where a great many Turks were on their knees worshipping their God. I gave a banknote to an elderly lady sitting on the pavement outside the mosque with a begging bowl in her lap. We ended our day by having a late lunch on one of the gaily-coloured tables outside a waterfront cafe.

I booked a day trip to an ancient Roman town some miles away and was amazed to see some of the buildings were still intact. My admirer came along too and took a few more snaps of me. The local guide told us his village had been without water for over a month.

I also booked a night trip to health-giving under-water caves with six other club members, including my admirer. Shortly after dinner we were taken by a minibus to Bodrum where we boarded a small boat that took us out to sea and dropped anchor alongside some rocks. We removed our top clothing, revealing our swimwear, and climbed out of the boat onto the rocks. We slid into a passageway between the rocks and waded through waist-high seawater. The guide went ahead and lit several large torches inside the caves as by now we were in darkness. I didn't like being in the water as we were a fair distance from the shore and I wondered what else was in it. Once inside the caves I climbed onto the rocks and stayed there despite several calls of 'Come on down, Sylvia.' Everyone else remained in the water, some boasting they were urinating.

One of the women noticed something swim into the cave and called out, 'What was that?'

The guide replied, 'It was only a large fish and it's gone now.' I climbed even higher above the rocks and remained there until it was time to return to the boat. My admirer very kindly came to my rescue. Ahead of the others he led me through the watery passageway onto the rocks and back into the boat. As I wanted to change into my dry clothes I said to him, 'Close your eyes.'

He was astounded and repeated, 'Close your eyes!'

I thought to myself, 'The world has gone mad.'

Soon my holiday came to an end. Those who were leaving left large tips to the staff of the villa. The coach drove us to the airport. As we crossed the tarmac I saw several Turkish soldiers armed with machine guns. Once the plane door was shut behind us the stewardesses warned everyone to remove any contact lenses or spectacles and then proceeded to spray the aircraft with insecticide. I noticed we were all seated together.

An hour into the flight I saw another plane in the distance. I asked a stewardess, 'Are we supposed to see other planes?'

She bent down and looked out the window and replied, 'It's perfectly normal to see lots of other aircraft. And that plane is probably several miles away from us.'

Jan called out from the seat in front of mine, 'Go back to sleep, Sylvia.'

We had a smooth flight and landed safely at Heathrow Airport. Despite exchanging telephone numbers I have not had any contact with any club member since the holiday.

sixteen

Brighton

– 1989 –

Ginnie and I had met two years previously on the singles holiday in Puddyford, Devon. We became friends and on our return to London we would socialize and occasionally visit seaside towns at weekends. We decided to spend the August Bank Holiday weekend in Brighton, a seaside town on the south coast of England. On the Thursday evening before the holiday I telephoned various guest houses in Brighton and found a few priced at £15 per person for bed and breakfast. I phoned Ginnie and asked if I could book one but she preferred to leave it until we were in Brighton as she felt she could find cheaper.

On the Saturday morning we caught the 8 a.m. train from Victoria Station, London, travelling direct to Brighton. On our arrival at the resort we spent some considerable time walking through the streets whilst carrying our suitcases looking for accommodation. We eventually found a guest house whose rate was £12.50 per person for a twin-bedded room with breakfast. Ginnie decided we should stay. The guest house was terraced and five storeys high. It was in a side street off the front and was run by two middle-aged Polish men. The breakfast room was on the ground floor but there was no bar. We climbed the stairs to our room on the second floor and unpacked. The bathroom was further down the hall and shared by the other tenants on that floor. We spent the remainder of the day sightseeing.

In the evening we had dinner in a wine bar. At 9.30 p.m. I said to Ginnie, 'I'm really tired. Can we go back to the hotel?'

She replied, 'Well, all right, but I don't think much of going away for the weekend and you want to go to bed this early.'

I didn't argue but I thought to myself, 'I've been working hard all week, we had an early start and traipsing around Brighton with our luggage for a couple of hours because you're too tight to spend some money has more or less finished me off.'

We returned to the guest house. As Ginnie didn't

like me smoking cigarettes I agreed not to smoke in the bedroom but to open the door and exhale into the hallway. Our accommodation could have been cleaner but the house was in the condition I would expect with two men running it by themselves. Ginnie was not satisfied her bed linen was clean. She went downstairs and complained to the manager and returned with fresh sheets and pillowcases. She said, 'If there's anything wrong with my breakfast in the morning I'm going to ask for my money back.'

Around 1 a.m. we were woken by several drunken girls returning to the room opposite ours. They were shrieking and laughing and joking in the hallway for several minutes before entering their room and slamming their bedroom door. We considered it unwise to complain to them as we felt we could have had an unpleasant argument, but we did complain to the manager in the morning. He apologized but told us, 'This is a holiday town.' Fortunately our English breakfast was acceptable so Ginnie said no more to him.

As the weather was warm and sunny Ginnie and I decided to walk along the front to see the new housing marina at the edge of the resort. We passed the famous nudist beach. Ginnie said to me, 'I'm going to have a look at this lot.' She walked across the stony beach weaving her way through the nudists whilst I looked on from the safe distance of the pavement. I clearly saw several nude men walking over the pebbles and a few couples sitting on beach towels, all of whom were totally unfazed by their nudity and the stares from the passers-by. We eventually reached the marina and lunched in its pub. In the afternoon we visited the famous streets called the Lanes with their antique shops. We spent some time window-shopping and ended the day by dining and drinking in a pub until late in the evening.

The following morning we were unable to use the bathroom as it was continuously engaged. We decided to have a shower in the shower room on the ground floor, which contained two separate showers. Ginnie was the first down but she was unable to work either appliance. She asked the manager for assistance. I arrived with my toilet bag and bath towel when he had just repaired the first shower. I walked straight into the cubicle, leaving Ginnie to wait whilst the manager repaired the remaining one. She made no comment until we were both in our bedroom. She was furious and yelled at me, 'I should have been the first in the shower! You saw me sorting it out with the manager and you just come along and walk into it leaving me to wait for him to fix the next one. You've got a bloody cheek! I don't think you'd like it if I did that to you!' Ginnie was quite right. I shouldn't have done that but I didn't realize until after I had entered the cubicle, and I didn't like being shouted at. I was very annoyed. I lit a cigarette and placed it in the ashtray whilst I dressed and smoked openly in the room. I went down to breakfast and lit another cigarette at the dining table. Ginnie arrived a few minutes later and asked the manager, 'Is there another table I can sit on, because I don't like cigarette smoke.'

He replied, 'If you ask your friend to put it out I'm sure she will.'

Ginnie replied, 'I don't think so.'

I stubbed out the cigarette and Ginnie sat opposite me at the table. We did not speak. After breakfast we both returned to the bedroom. I did not smoke in the room but slowly packed my suitcase whilst Ginnie sat on the bed applying her make-up. She said, 'Don't bother waiting for me. I'm going to be ages yet.'

I said, 'OK.' I locked my suitcase and left the hotel. I walked down to the front and sat on one of the sheltered seats overlooking the sea and lunched in a nearby fish restaurant. I returned to the train station an hour before our train was due and sat on one of the benches. I saw Ginnie enter the station. She must have seen me but chose to walk straight past me without glancing in my direction. I did not see her on the train and we have had no further contact since that holiday.

seventeen

Blackpool

– 1991 –

Sandra was a twenty-two-year-old Northern Irish woman whom I met when she and her childhood friend Shaunagh shared a room in the same furnished house I lived in. Despite being over twenty years older than both girls, the three of us became friends and had great fun together. At the time of our holiday Sandra was a bus conductress whilst I was unemployed. Also I had moved out of the house we had shared.

It was February and Sandra had a week off and suggested the two of us should have a short holiday in the UK. Shaunagh was unable to come with us because she was working. I chose Blackpool, a seaside town in the north-west of England, as a pleasant place to spend a winter break and Sandra agreed with me. I made all the arrangements, booking the coach from Victoria Coach Station and for the home journey five days later. I telephoned Directory Enquiries and asked the operator to give me the telephone number of a few hotels in Blackpool and I found a small family-run guest house five minutes' walk from the sea.

I was under the impression that Sandra thought I was very entertaining company and that we'd have a hilarious five days. I said to her, 'Don't expect to have a laugh on this holiday because it's winter. It's going to be cold and windy and I should think half of Blackpool is closed until the summer. We'll just have some fresh air and a relaxing time. And I don't suppose we're going to meet any men either.' Despite saying this I don't think Sandra paid attention to me.

We boarded the coach at Victoria Coach Station and set off for Blackpool. We started off very chatty but halfway up the motorway our conversation began to ebb and we drifted into silence. Unfortunately a four-year-old boy sitting behind us with his mother continually kicked the backs of our seats, which didn't please Sandra. Eventually I turned round and politely asked the young mother to stop the child from doing so. I was met with silence and an icy stare but the kicking stopped, which temporarily revived the conversation between me and Sandra.

On our arrival in Blackpool's coach station we hired a cab to take us to the guest house. A young woman in her thirties met us and showed us to our room, which was on the first floor. It was twin-bedded, containing a washbasin. The bathroom was further down the hall and we were to discover that we shared it with the family. There were no other lodgers staying there.

Our landlady invited us to the family lounge on the ground floor for a cup of tea. She introduced herself as Janet. She was very friendly and told us she had three school-age daughters, that she was a 'dinner lady' at the local school and her husband worked on the railways. The lounge was also a breakfast room. Janet invited us to watch TV and have a coffee with the family at the end of our day. The house comprised a basement, ground and two upper floors, with six rooms available for bed and breakfast. Janet told us the children slept in the basement and that the marital bedroom was the room adjacent to the kitchen on the ground floor. She also said she and her husband had a holiday every year so that they had a 'break from the children'.

It was now mid-afternoon and Sandra and I had not eaten since an early breakfast. We walked to the front where we found a suitable restaurant and had lunch. I spoke to Sandra as we ate. Her reply was, 'Mmmmmmm.' Then we explored Blackpool's 'Golden Mile' of amusement houses. As I expected only a few were open. Most of the others were boarded up and some were being painted. We saw the famous tower. It didn't look very exciting on a grey winter's day. The vast beach was sandy and free of stones. There were plenty of people about but few holidaymakers. I heard the sound of northern accents all around me. I noticed the women frequently wore white ankle socks and flat shoes with skirts and dresses. The weather was cold and windy. I chatted to Sandra as we walked. My every attempt at conversation was met with the reply, 'Mmmmmmm.' I eventually stopped talking. We looked around the many shops. I entered a stationer's to buy writing paper and envelopes and some birthday cards, thinking they might be different to those on sale in London. They weren't. Sandra moaned, 'You can buy all of this stuff in London.' In the evening we had a fish dinner and then went into a pub, to find we were the barman's only customers throughout this time. I chatted to Sandra but her response was 'Mmmmmmm' and she did not try to make any conversation. Once again I stopped talking. After two drinks and silence between us we returned to the guest house. It was 9.30 p.m.

Sandra complained, 'I don't think much of going back at this time.'

I replied, 'What else is there to do?' She didn't answer me. We walked back to the guest house. I attempted conversation. Sandra would reply, 'Mmmmmmm.' We joined Janet and her family in the lounge.

After an excellent breakfast the following morning Sandra and I again walked to the front. I suggested, 'Why don't we go for a walk on the pier?'

'Oh, no,' she moaned, 'my hair will be ruined.'

I suggested, 'Why don't we have a walk on the beach and see where it leads us to?'

She replied, 'No. It's too windy and my hair will look a mess.'

I looked at Sandra's dark long curls and thought, 'Why not put a scarf over your head or buy some hair clips.' We walked around the amusement houses and joined in a game of bingo. Sandra won a game and chose a small china cat as her prize. We entered a souvenir shop and bought some presents for friends at home and some postcards. During this time I spoke to Sandra but was met with 'Mmmmmmm' at my every attempt at conversation. Lunchtime we had a sandwich and a coffee in a large bakery. Sandra sat at the table writing her postcards. I picked one up and read 'I'm having a lovely time . . .' I thought to myself, 'I don't think you are.'

In the afternoon we came across a theatre. As there was no other suitable entertainment we booked two seats for the evening performance. We continued exploring the back streets of Blackpool. We had an argument at a set of traffic lights. Sandra pointed and said, 'That car went through a red light.'

I replied, 'It didn't. There's a green filter light for those who want to turn left.'

She lost her temper and shouted, 'That isn't right, Sylvia!'

I didn't argue further and we walked in silence. After dinner in a cafe along the front we went to see a very uninteresting play. During the interval we had a drink at the bar. I tried conversation again. Sandra's reply was, 'Mmmmmmm.'

The following morning we took the train to Liverpool. I was amazed to see a town similar to the heart of London, full of historic buildings and a large museum. We leaned on the concrete wall overlooking the River Mersey and saw the ferry. We fed the pigeons. Sandra asked a passer-by if he knew where the TV soap *Brookside* was being filmed. He replied, 'It's too far away for you to get to.'

I said to Sandra, 'I think I'll go in that museum for about an hour and I'll meet you at the bench outside, if that's all right?'

'What do you want to go in there for?' she queried.

After the museum we had lunch in a busy pub full of smartly dressed people. I decided they were office workers in their lunch break. I chatted to Sandra. Her response was, 'Mmmmmmm.'

We caught a train to Blackpool about 5 p.m. and returned to the guest house, spending the remainder of the evening with Janet and her family in their lounge. We went to bed in silence.

Before breakfast the following morning Sandra said to me, 'I'm going back to London on the next coach. Can I have the tickets, Sylvia? I'll have them changed.'

I was still in bed. I reached for my handbag and gave her our tickets, saying, 'Don't alter my one.'

She replied, 'I won't do anything to yours, Sylvia. I'll give it to you when I come back.' She returned in time for breakfast and gave me my new ticket. I left the house as she began to pack.

I spent the day walking along the beach and exploring the streets further along the front. I had lunch and dinner in Blackpool cafes. In the evening I returned to the lounge and Janet and her family. Janet asked me, 'Why did Sandra leave so early?'

I replied, 'I think she thought she was going to have a really good laugh and then found she didn't.'

The next morning I packed my small suitcase. I looked around the room to make sure I hadn't missed anything. I was surprised to see Sandra's china cat sitting on the window ledge. I picked it up and took it with me when I left the house. On the way to the coach station I passed a church and saw a sign over the main door saying 'Jumble Wanted'. I placed the china cat beside two black dustbins resting against the church door. After lunch I took my last look at Blackpool and boarded the coach to London mid-afternoon.

When I saw Shaunagh some days later I asked her, 'What did Sandra say about Blackpool?'

'Nothing,' she replied.

eighteen

Ramsgate

– 1996 to 2000 –

I met Tim at a dinner held by a social club we had both recently joined. He sat opposite me at the table and soon engaged me in conversation. I was very flattered when he remarked, 'You must have a lot of trouble with men.' I would see Tim at various events. He frequently asked me out but I declined his offers. I'd joined the club because I'd had a long-term relationship end and I was upset about it. At that time I was very close to my cousin June and we would discuss each other's problems. I told her about Tim and, as she didn't like my ex-boyfriend and hoped we would stay apart, she said, 'Go out with Tim and give him a chance. You might find you like him and also cheer yourself up.' I decided June was right and the next time Tim asked me out

I accepted the invitation. This proved to be the beginning of a friendship that spanned four years.

Tim was in his forties and eight years my junior. He was a skilled worker on a building site and had a cockney accent. He was five feet ten inches tall and dark haired. He owned a very old car and told me, 'My car is so reliable I couldn't part with it.'

On our first date Tim drove me to Southend, a seaside town thirty miles outside London. We visited the Planetarium and watched an interesting video of the night sky. We lunched in British Home Stores and walked along the front. We passed a Mothercare shop and looked at the prams, making a few light-hearted comments. Tim's final comment was, 'As you're past fifty I don't reckon you can fill one of those!'

On our second date Tim came round to my flat for a coffee. Halfway through the evening he said, 'I'm thinking of buying a delicatessen and cafe in Surrey. Would you be interested in helping me run the business and living with me in the flat above it?'

I replied, 'Tim, I'm sorry but I don't think we will ever be anything other than friends, but thank you for the offer.'

Despite my reply Tim continued to see me. He took me at my word and did not make any passes at me. One evening he phoned and said, 'I usually motor down to Ramsgate every Sunday to see my mother. She owns a cottage there. Would you like to come with me this Sunday?' I was very pleased and accepted his invitation.

Tim decided not to buy the delicatessen.

Tim picked me up at 8 a.m. every Sunday that summer and we would drive on the motorway to Ramsgate. We usually stopped for a cooked breakfast and Tim would fill the car with petrol at a well-known supermarket, using my card to collect the credits. I paid for the breakfasts and Tim would treat me to dinner later in the day. I did not pay for the petrol. Tim was a safe driver, rarely going faster than 60 m.p.h. and staying in the slow lane. We would chat as we travelled. He must have taken that route countless times before but our conversations would distract him and we frequently found ourselves in the wrong lane, which would usually take us twenty minutes out of our way. He would tell me it was my fault.

We would arrive at his mother's home around noon. Her name was Edith. She was slim, grey haired and in her mid-seventies. She walked with the aid of a walking stick. Edith was always very kind and polite to me. I slowly discovered she had a wicked sense of humour and was quite modern in her approach to life. Although she was a smoker she would not allow smoking in the cottage. The three of us would smoke in the back garden, resting against window ledges, using an empty tin as our ashtray.

Tim would drive us to a restaurant with a view of the coastline of the small seaside town in south-east England. Sometimes he would drive us to Broadstairs or Margate, towns further along the coast. As Edith was unable to walk too far we would occasionally leave her in the car overlooking the sea until our return. I remember those times as pleasant Sundays spent with friends.

In the autumn I told Tim I didn't want to see so much of him and our Sundays ceased. As I was good friends with Edith I would phone her every week. I saw Tim occasionally. He invited me to Ramsgate just before one Christmas and suggested I stay overnight, sleeping in the spare bedroom. I accepted his offer.

Tim picked me up at 8 a.m. as usual and we motored down the motorway. For some weeks I had noticed a red light flickering on the dashboard. I would tell Tim. He would reply, 'It's only the water pump. Sometimes the light goes off. We've got

plenty of water so perhaps the light's up the creek.'
We were thirty miles from Ramsgate. Suddenly Tim
said, 'There's something wrong with the car! It's
slowing up and I can't get any power out of it! I'll
have to pull over to the hard shoulder and phone
the AA.' This he did, using his mobile phone. An
AA van arrived half an hour later. After inspecting
Tim's car the AA mechanic said, 'You're completely
out of oil. This car has seized up. It's no good to
anyone and you'll have to scrap it.'

Tim said, 'I thought it was a faulty water-pump
light on the dashboard.'

The mechanic replied, 'No, that must have been
the oil light.'

Tim turned to me and said, 'Why couldn't you
tell me it was the oil light?'

I replied, 'Don't blame me! You're the one who
said it was the water pump.'

He added, 'Yes, but if you look clearly at the
dashboard you can see it's an oil can and the water
pump doesn't look like that at all.'

I replied, 'Tim. You had that oil light flickering
away for weeks and you ignored it. You've just
ruined your own car and it's nothing to do with
me.'

The AA man interrupted our discussion and said

to Tim, 'I'll attach you to a tow rope and you just steer your car behind me. I'll take you to the next service station, which is about seventeen miles away.'

We soon set off. Unfortunately the AA man drove up the motorway at fifty miles an hour. Tim shouted at me, 'This steering wheel is wobbling about all over the place and it's difficult to hang on to. I hope he doesn't suddenly slow down!'

We reached the service station safely. The AA man came over to us and said, 'You'll have a breakdown truck arrive soon to take you the rest of your journey.' We got out of the car and went for a coffee. By this time Tim saw the funny side. Eventually the breakdown truck arrived. The driver attached Tim's ruined car to the back of his vehicle and we climbed into his cabin. We were driven direct to Edith's street door in full view of her neighbours. The following day Tim paid a car breaker to dispose of his car and we returned to London by coach in the late afternoon.

In the February, Tim decided to spend a year travelling around Asia. He had been there before and told me life out there was considerably cheaper than in the UK. Whilst he was overseas he wrote me letters and sent me postcards of the places he had visited. He would phone Edith every few weeks and we would relay messages. During his absence I travelled by coach to Ramsgate to spend a few days with Edith, using minicabs to take us to places of interest. On his return to the UK, Tim met me in London and gave me a silk dressing gown, a watch and two unusual cigarette lighters as a present. As he had nowhere else to live he stayed with Edith in Ramsgate. He was unable to find suitable work there so he contacted an agency and was soon sent as a temporary worker on building sites in various parts of the UK. Suddenly Edith's health deteriorated. Tim phoned me from Glasgow and asked if I'd stay with her for a few days to keep her company and do the housework she was now unable to do and he would pay for my trip. I booked a coach for the following Monday.

On the Sunday I visited my elderly parents. They were in good health. I told them, 'I'm going to Ramsgate tomorrow to stay with Edith for a few days. I'll phone you Wednesday and I'll be back on Thursday.' The following day I knocked on Edith's street door just after 3 p.m. I found her in good spirits but very forgetful, sometimes confused, and unable to walk very far. It was June but the weather was awful. It poured with rain non-stop and was very windy. I thoroughly enjoyed cleaning the cottage, taking the minicab to do the shopping and cooking our food, but the weather was so bad we couldn't go out anywhere. I decided to return to London late Wednesday. When I arrived in my flat I played my answerphone. I froze as I recognized the voice of one of my parents' neighbours requesting me to phone home urgently. I did so and spoke to my mother. She said, 'Sylvie, I'm sorry to have to tell you, dear, but poor old Dad died of a massive heart attack on Monday afternoon.' It was a terrible shock. It had not occurred to me to leave Edith's address or telephone number.

Tim was forced to return to Ramsgate because of Edith's ill health. She was no longer able to shop. He would take whatever job he could find there. He phoned me and said, 'I've just taken a job picking tomatoes. The only problem is I'm a bit colour-blind and the boss wants bright orange tomatoes only and I can't distinguish them from the others. So I'm filling up the boxes with any old tomatoes and then I'm picking what I think are bright orange ones and laying them on top of the others and I'm hoping the boss won't notice.' Needless to say the boss did notice and Tim's job lasted precisely ten days.

As I was unemployed and my days were free Tim began inviting me to Ramsgate for several days at a time. He asked me to do all the housework and cooking and in return he would pay for my holiday. This was a very good bargain and very nice of him. He paid for my fares from my street door and for my food. I usually went down there on a Friday and he would pay for a day trip to Calais on the Shuttle over the weekend, supplying me with £10 worth of French francs and treating me to my duty-free shopping. I would travel to Ramsgate with £51 in my purse and would return to London with £41 remaining five days later.

Edith spent her days sitting in her armchair by the fire in the lounge watching TV. She was as cheerful as ever. When I said how good Tim was to me she laughed and replied, 'Everyone likes Tim until he loses his temper.'

I was about to wash the telephone. I said to Edith, 'A few months ago I washed my telephone with disinfectant and I used so much water that when I pressed the buttons water oozed out and I had to buy another phone. The BT lady said, "Well, at least you didn't put it in the washing machine." '

Edith laughed but said, 'I don't want my one washed, thank you.' I promised I wouldn't do the same thing twice and let Edith test the damp cloth before I cleaned her phone.

Tim would take me for long walks from his mother's home, through the park and down to the seafront, where we frequently enjoyed a breakfast in a cafe just off the harbour with its gay sailing boats. At other times he would take me along the coastline away from the town, over shrubland with the sea beside us. Of an evening we would stay in the cottage with Edith watching television. If Tim was working during the week I would take a minicab to the town centre and wander through the numerous shops.

At Tim's request I made several trips to Ramsgate, each one totally financed by him and in return I would do the housework and the cooking. He invited me down every month but I spaced out the holidays to every six or seven weeks. We always had a day trip to Calais. I was of the opinion that he was serious about me. He would say, 'I just like your company.' Most of the time he was working, sometimes as a carer in a nursing home, which he would describe as 'a bum job'. Eventually he bought another car and asked if he could holiday in London with me. I housed him in my old bedroom at my mother's house overnight, spending time in my furnished flat during the day. Tim made several trips to London but I was not to travel to Ramsgate again. Every time Tim came to London he would really annoy me. If he didn't feel very well he thought it was perfectly acceptable to snap at me all day. If I served him a glass of beer he would drink only half and the remainder would go down the sink. If I cooked his dinner he always left some of it. He would also spend his time biting his fingernails despite me telling him it really irritated me. We even started rowing. On his return to Ramsgate he began phoning me several times each week. I would say to him, 'Tim, you're a mate of mine. You're not my boyfriend so don't phone me more than once a week.' He paid no attention to my complaints and telephoned me when it suited him. Sometimes he would phone me as much as three times a day. This behaviour really upset me. I kept complaining but allowed the situation to continue for around three months because we had been such good friends, but in the end he became a nuisance caller and I asked BT to change my telephone number.

nineteen

Rome

- 1999 -

My friend Jenny and I decided to spend Easter of that year in Rome, a city neither one of us had visited before. Jenny was tall and blonde and three years younger than me. We met when I became a lodger in the house she owned. We scoured the daily newspapers for the cheapest package. With my agreement, Jenny booked a twin-bedded room with a bathroom, and breakfast for three nights with return air travel from Gatwick airport for the sum of £299, travelling early on the Good Friday and returning to the UK on the Monday evening. This enabled us to have four full days in Rome. Jenny arranged for a minicab to take us to the airport at 5 a.m. to catch a 7 a.m. flight on the Good Friday and booked the cab for the return journey. We arrived at Gatwick with time to spare and both bought a breakfast. We also had time to buy various items from the duty-free shop.

There were no delays or queues at the airport as there are occasionally at Easter and we boarded the plane at the scheduled time. We had a smooth flight. I sat by the window enjoying the view whilst Jenny read a newspaper. We were met in Rome by a young female Italian courier who spoke fluent English. We boarded the waiting coach with approximately twenty other tourists and were driven to our hotel.

As we entered reception we were disappointed to see approximately thirty people surrounded by luggage waiting to be given a hotel room. We sat at the back of the room with our suitcases and watched the male receptionist as he telephoned various hotels. He frequently buried his head in his hands and we realized there was a serious problem. Suddenly our courier began to hand out room keys to those nearest her. I said to Jenny, 'Wait here and I'll see if I can get one of those keys.' I walked across the room to the desk.

The courier held out another key, saying, 'Twin-bedded room on the first floor.'

I reached out and took the key from her, saying, 'Thank you.' Heaving a sigh of relief I returned to

Jenny. We picked up our suitcases and made our way to our hotel room.

We entered a beautiful twin-bedded room over-looking the street. It was very elegant with expensive counterpanes and matching curtains and a highly polished mirror covering the entire wall behind the two beds. A mahogany desk with a TV on top had a fridge built into it and faced the beds. The bathroom included a bidet and hairdryer. We began to unpack. The telephone rang. Jenny answered. From the conversation I could hear I gathered that reception had changed their mind about our room and wanted us to move elsewhere.

I said to Jenny, 'Tell them no. We're quite happy with this room.'

Jenny ignored my comment and I heard her say, 'All right, we'll move to the next floor and I'll come down and exchange the keys.' I wasn't very pleased but made no comment.

Our room on the second floor was extremely elegant but unfortunately it contained a double bed. I said to Jenny, 'There's no way I'm sharing that bed.'

She replied, 'I quite agree with you! I'll go down to reception and tell them this is unsuitable and we'll have our old room back.' I heard a heated discussion and Jenny's voice shouting up the stair-well for some ten minutes. She eventually returned to our double room and said, 'Come on, we're going back into the other room.'

I asked, 'Why did they want us to change in the first place?'

She replied, 'They were trying to sort out a family with two children. Reception wanted our room for the parents and the room next door for the children. Now the people the other side of the children's room are moving elsewhere and the parents are going in there instead as it's got a double bed.' We returned to our beautiful twin-bedded room, unpacked, put our flat shoes on and decided to have lunch and do some sightseeing, much later than we had intended.

As we were hungry we lunched in an Italian res-taurant a few yards from the hotel and ate a delicious salad. We bought a map from a tobacco-nist. I left Jenny in charge of our sightseeing and we spent the remainder of the day walking. In the evening we visited the Colosseum and were told by other tourists that a service was going be held with the Pope in attendance. A large crowd gathered and we joined them as darkness fell. After an hour or so of standing on our aching feet, hymn books and lighted candles were given out to enable us to read. We joined in the singing but as time passed by we realized the Pope was not going to appear so we walked through the crowd and dined in a nearby restaurant and eventually walked back to our hotel.

Jenny and I woke around 7 a.m. each morning. Neither one of us stayed in bed. I was usually the first up. After a visit to the bathroom I would open the window wide and lean over the sill in my night-dress smoking my first cigarette of the day as Jenny was a non-smoker and didn't like the smell of smoke in the bedroom. When I finished my cigarette I would comb my hair, put a dress on and then hurry downstairs to the dining room for a longed-for cup of coffee, whilst Jenny showered and dressed. On my return Jenny would go to breakfast as I got ready for the day. After two days of almost nonstop walking I suggested we should travel by tram or the underground to save our feet. Despite doing so we were still extremely active. We usually returned to the hotel around midnight. I would climb into bed with the soles of my feet aching and I would fre-quently fall asleep whilst Jenny was talking to me.

I found Rome to be a beautiful city steeped in history. The Italian people were kind and friendly towards us. The weather was warm and sunny each day of our stay. Also Rome was much cheaper than London.

I chose to wear a black lace see-through top with a black bra underneath. I attracted so much attention from Italian men as I walked through the streets that I felt forced to put my jacket on. Whilst travelling on the trams Jenny and I accidentally 'pulled' two elderly Italian men who smiled as they squeezed up against us in the crowded aisle where we were 'strap-hanging'. Jenny got into conversation with a young Italian man at the bus station who took her telephone number so he could call her the next time he was in London. (He never made the call.) That was the closest we got to romance during that holiday.

We saw most of the sights, ninety per cent of the time on foot. We threw coins in the Trevi Fountain and made our wishes. Jenny said, 'We must buy an ice cream from the shop beside the fountain as someone in the office said it's the best ice cream in the world.' We bought two large cornets and agreed with her colleague's comment.

Unfortunately for me the people of Rome are not very keen on cigarette smoking. We usually dined in the restaurant near the hotel. As soon as I lit a cigarette and asked for an ashtray the party at the next table would politely complain. Because of this we changed tables three times in one evening. Jenny took these moves with great good humour. Fortunately no one stopped me from smoking in the fresh air as I sat on the steps of the historic buildings.

One day shortly after breakfast we decided to visit Julius Caesar's palace. After paying my admission at the kiosk I discovered we would be walking in the open air as the palace and its grounds were almost reduced to rubble. I looked in my handbag for a cigarette only to find I had left the packet in my hotel room. The ticket clerk allowed me to go through the barrier to find a tobacconist but there were none in sight. Empty-handed I returned to Jenny who laughed and said, 'This is one of the few places you can smoke and you forget your cigarettes.' It was 3.45 p.m. before I managed to buy cigarettes and have my third one that day.

One evening after an early dinner we joined a coach party on a spectacular night-time trip around Rome where we were taken to all the tourist areas. As the coach was only half full we chose separate seats to enable us both to sit by a window. I was grateful not to be on foot.

On the Easter Sunday we took the tram to St

Peter's Square. It was filled with tourists. We could see the Pope in the distance sitting on a dais surrounded by Church officials. It was a very hot day and we moved with difficulty through the crowd. We took it in turns to stand on a low wall where we could see the Pope more clearly, but Jenny tired of the struggle to stand and suggested we leave. Later that day I heard the Pope gave a blessing soon after we left and on my return to London I read in a newspaper that he gave a speech on Kosovo. I was very disappointed to have missed both events.

I didn't buy too many souvenirs on this holiday as my funds were running low. The only present I bought was for my mother. Jenny didn't have this problem and spent freely. She bought two pairs of leather shoes, some jewellery, perfume and wine out of the duty-free shop and various videos and books on the Sistine Chapel and the Vatican. She also bought presents for her family and friends.

Soon our holiday came to a close. The coach returned us to the airport in time for an 8.30 p.m. flight. At Gatwick the minicab was waiting for us and I reached home shortly after 1 a.m. on the Tuesday morning. After all the exertions of the previous four days I decided to take things easy for the rest of the week. Jenny had the same intention but unfortunately her mother phoned at 8 a.m. on the Tuesday morning with errands for Jenny to see to and Jenny returned to the office on the Wednesday.

twenty

Gibraltar

- 1999 -

I met Susan at a social club outing some three years before we decided to travel to Gibraltar. We became very friendly and would often go to club events together. Also I would occasionally visit Susan's house in East London on a Saturday night to help her with the 'homework' she took in from a nearby factory.

We were both in our fifties. I was single. Susan was the divorced mother of three adult children and shared her home with her youngest daughter and the girl's fiancé. She was very overweight but had an attractive face and thick natural blonde hair, which she wore short. She eventually sold the house to the couple and moved to the coast. Susan invited me to her new home and I made several weekend trips, staying overnight and driving myself back to London around midday on the Sunday. During this time I found her to be a good friend, very polite and kind. We were both out of work but with some savings so we decided to go on a week's holiday together.

I collected an assortment of brochures from a local travel agent and leafed through the pages. I finally chose Gibraltar as a suitable destination and telephoned Susan. She obtained the same brochure from her travel agent and agreed with my choice. As our funds were limited we chose the first week in September as our departure date because it was considerably cheaper than a midsummer booking. We decided that I should make the arrangements. I phoned Susan many times as I sorted out the holiday, keeping her up to date with the latest position or seeking her approval. I noticed that I made eight telephone calls to the coast and she only made one to me. She did phone me from her daughter's house one weekend, which was approximately half a mile away and probably cost her nothing. She offered to phone the local minicab companies asking their prices then booking the cheapest return fare to the airport, which was originally my idea. I declined as it would only have cost about 30p and

I didn't trust her to do it right. I thought the lack of calls from the coast to be unfair and vowed to leave Susan to make the next call. It was three and a half weeks before our departure date. Also, I noticed Susan's manner was very argumentative on occasions. When I said something that could be taken two ways and added, 'Oh, I didn't mean it that way,' she would reply, 'Oh, yes, you did!' During another call she made the comment, 'No one tells me what to do.' I suddenly realized I had made a mistake. I thought over our relationship, the comments I had let go and her bursts of temper with other people, and concluded that she was not easy-going as I had thought but was far too aggressive and a willing party to an argument. I became apprehensive about the holiday but it was too late to cancel.

The days, then weeks, slowly passed with no contact from Susan. I told my friend Jenny. She asked, 'Who's got the tickets?'

'I have,' I replied.

She laughed and said, 'Well, she'll have to phone you otherwise she won't be able to go.'

I was determined not to be the one to break our silence and decided not to phone Susan until two days before the departure date. I had a slight shock when she phoned me a few days prior to that, without making any adverse comments.

The day before the holiday I woke to discover I had a severe head cold, a rasping chest and a blocked sinus. I didn't have the time to make an appointment with my doctor as I had last-minute shopping and my packing to see to. I phoned the surgery explaining my circumstances, asking if I could speak to him. My doctor obliged and told me a course of antibiotics was needed and he would leave a prescription for me to collect from reception when I was able. I added the chemist to my shopping list and finally collected my tablets, feeling very unwell and hoping they would have a magical effect.

As planned, Susan drove up from the coast and stayed overnight in her daughter's house. She arrived at my door with the minicab at 5 a.m. the following morning to take us to Gatwick Airport. My cold seemed worse and I didn't feel well at all. We chatted during the journey. On arrival at the airport the driver removed our suitcases from the boot of the car and I paid him the agreed £35 fare. Susan and I placed our suitcases by the seats immediately inside the glass doors. She said to me, 'You told me the minicab was only going to cost £30, not £35!'

I replied, 'No, I didn't.'

She replied, 'Oh, yes, you did!'

'No, I didn't,' I replied.

'Oh, yes, you did,' she repeated, adding, 'And you told me we were coming back on the 10th and not the 9th!'

I replied, 'No, I didn't. It's you that's in the muddle, not me.'

Our argument progressed into a heated exchange until Susan shouted, 'Shut up about it!'

I replied, 'Well, I didn't do anything of the sort!'

She yelled, 'Well, I think you did!'

I did not comment further.

Susan said, 'We'd better find out which gate we're supposed to go to.'

We picked up our suitcases, both of which were on wheels, and walked deeper into the airport. I followed her thinking to myself, 'We've just had a flaming great row and we haven't got on the plane yet.' We continued talking to one another as though nothing had happened and agreed to part as I wanted the cigarette department and Susan wanted perfumery, arranging to meet under the flight information board twenty minutes later.

We met up with one another at the same time as a loudspeaker called out, 'Would Smith and Thomas please report to Gate No. 2 immediately for GB Flight No. 267 to Gibraltar. This gate will close in five minutes' time.' We looked at each other in horror and ran through the corridors, our suitcases clattering behind us, until we found Gate No. 2, just in time to hand in our luggage and board the waiting coach taking us to the aeroplane. We had a smooth flight.

We landed on Gibraltar's tiny airstrip around lunchtime to find warm summer sunshine. Our hotel room was the standard twin bed with en suite bathroom, with a balcony overlooking the harbour. A coloured TV set sat on a wooden table facing the two single beds. Unfortunately we were immediately above a busy roundabout and the noise of the traffic was so loud we could hardly hear the TV. This did not prevent me from sleeping but Susan spent the first night wide awake as the traffic, mainly scooters, continued until the early hours. I said to her, 'If you want to see reception and change our room I'll back you.' Instead she chose to buy earplugs from a nearby pharmacy.

Susan didn't object to me smoking in the bedroom. Also she said, 'I'll leave a box of matches in the bathroom for us to use when we do number twos. You just light a match and leave it to burn and it burns up all the smells.' I tried it out and found she was right.

Breakfast was always the same each morning, consisting of orange juice, cereal, fried egg, bacon and tomato, and plenty of coffee. This was cooked by Sam, a Moroccan barman, and served by Happy. Happy was a short, middle-aged, extremely rotund Gibraltarian waiter, who wore squeaky shoes and a mournful expression which deepened when asked to do something. He was easily upset. One morning I sat at a table for four by myself. Happy looked very put out and asked me to move to a smaller table, which I did. Late one evening I phoned the bar requesting a pot of tea from Happy, who was acting barman as Sam had the evening off. Happy told me it was far too late for tea but I could come down and collect it. I politely cancelled my order. Fifteen minutes later there was a knock on the door. I opened it to see Happy with my tea tray.

We spent busy days sightseeing but of an evening we found nothing to do other than sit in a pub. After dinner we chose to return to the hotel and its bar but would find only Sam there. So we would retire to our room to watch TV. Despite this I enjoyed my holiday. I liked Gibraltar. I liked the climate, its people and its history. Gibraltar used to belong to Spain but from the beginning of the eighteenth century it has been under British rule. The currency is sterling. The local money is simply more colourful. Each day I telephoned my mother in London, placing a £1 coin in the slot of a street telephone and receiving five minutes' conversation for my money. Cigarettes and alcohol were considerably cheaper. We also found plenty of bargains in the shops and I noticed a branch of Marks & Spencer in the High Street. The traffic was nonstop. Both Susan and I wondered where everyone was travelling to because Gibraltar is only six square miles in size.

We took the cable car to the top of the famous Rock and found a restaurant and souvenir shop there. We had an excellent lunch and enjoyed spectacular views of the coastline with the Mediterranean Sea many metres below us. We had hoped to see the Barbary apes that roamed freely over the upper half of the Rock but unfortunately they were in their den some fifty feet lower down. I noticed the road to the den was one continuous sheer drop. I don't like heights, they make me dizzy, so I suggested to Susan, 'Why don't you walk down to the apes' den, because heights don't affect you as they do me. If I was you I'd go for it and I'll meet you back at the hotel.' This we did.

Susan and I booked a day trip to Morocco through a Gibraltarian travel agent. A minibus collected us from our hotel early in the morning and we joined other tourists on a journey to the Spanish coast. We boarded a ferry to North Africa where we were met by an elderly Moroccan guide called Mustapha. We climbed aboard a second minibus which drove to the Moroccan border. The Moroccan customs officials kept our passports. They were not returned until our home journey in the evening.

Mustapha claimed to speak many languages, taking it in turns to speak to the group in English, German and French. He told us this part of Morocco was very poor and pointed out the shacks and tents on the beach where some people were forced to live. He said the Moroccan government had recently passed a law stating that all children must attend school, in the hope of overcoming the poverty trap. I noticed fields covered in litter with the fierce African sun beating down, obviously creating germs and becoming potentially disease-ridden.

Our first stop was obviously pre-arranged. The

minibus came to a halt in a small field where several men were waiting with camels for the tourists to ride in exchange for pesetas. Susan bravely climbed aboard a large camel while I photographed her.

Our next stop was Tetouan. It seemed to me that we entered a huge rabbit warren of tunnels and apartments carved out of a large hill. Mustapha led the way with the group following. He took us through continuous passageways where there were stalls and shops especially for the tourists. Several men tried to sell us their wares. I turned down a set of bongo drums and various leather goods and 'silverware'. We walked passed rooms where children were working, sewing leather clothing. Mustapha brought our attention to a woman filling a bucket with water from a communal tap. He told us that she did not have running water in her apartment. I concluded that she had no bathroom or toilet in her home and assumed there had to be a cesspit somewhere.

Mustapha stopped at a large linenware stall where an elderly woman was serving. I whispered to Susan, 'She's probably his wife.' Susan and I examined the linen but none of it interested us. We moved to a stall a few feet away that was selling kaftans. We compared them to the ones in London but we didn't buy any. Some minutes later we turned round to rejoin the group only to discover they were not there. Susan uttered, 'Oh no!' We ran to the entrances of the many passageways looking for our party but we couldn't find them. Susan panicked, saying, 'Now what do we do?' Much to her annoyance I burst out laughing. I didn't blame her for panicking but I thought our situation was hysterically funny. Despite my laughter I was very pleased when 'Bongo Drums' came up to us. He realized what had happened and said, 'Do not worry. I know where Mustapha takes the tourists and I will take you to him. You follow me.' I trusted him totally and thought to myself, 'We are now saved.' Susan on the other hand was very upset. 'Bongo Drums' led us through passageway after passageway. My trust in him wavered slightly as he wandered away from the tourist area into a dimly lit residential part but was restored when we returned to the bright tourist passageways. After six minutes of following 'Bongo Drums' we stopped outside a large store selling pottery, leatherware, jewellery and carpets. He spoke in Arabic to the three men inside, then to us, saying, 'I will find Mustapha and tell him you are here.' He then left.

The three storekeepers invited us inside to have

a look at their wares. Both Susan and I declined as the shop was empty and the passageway deserted. Soon we were offered orange juice. Then two stools were placed in the doorway for our use. After such kindness I relaxed completely and decided the storekeepers were extremely nice people. Susan remained in the doorway whilst I entered the store, looking at their goods and eventually haggling over prices. Some twenty minutes later 'Bongo Drums' reappeared with Mustapha and the other tourists. Susan, quite rightly in my opinion, was absolutely furious that Mustapha had lost us and told him so in no uncertain terms.

'Bongo Drums' hovered around us saying, 'Something for me? Something for me?'

Susan snapped, 'Can't anybody do something for nothing!'

I saw his point of view. He was quite obviously poor and he had 'saved our lives'. I said to Susan, 'I'll give him some money.' Reluctant to give him a £5 note with no return I said to him, 'Will £5 cover the cost of your bongo drums?' He said nothing, gave me the drums, took the £5 note out of my hand and left the shop whilst Susan continued her argument with Mustapha.

Our day continued with lunch in the 'rabbit

warren' then a trip to Tangier, but I noticed Mustapha had employed a young man to make sure no one was left behind. If I stopped to look in a shop window and the group moved, he would hurry me along. At the end of our day our passports were returned as we drove through the Moroccan customs. Despite my experience I thoroughly enjoyed our excursion!

The following day Susan and I crossed the border into Spain and spent our time sightseeing. In the evening we returned to Gibraltar and walked down its High Street looking for a suitable restaurant. We had been walking for some time when Susan suddenly lost her temper and shouted, 'Well I don't want to go any further but I suppose you do so I'm going to be forced to!'

I didn't like this remark at all. I replied, 'I'm not forcing you to do anything, so I don't think you should cut up nasty about it!' My comment annoyed Susan further. She snapped at me again. I thought to myself, 'Oh, we're going to have a row, are we? How about I try to be three times nastier than you.' I saw a sign for bar food halfway up an alley and said, 'We could stop there, if that suits you!' We climbed the hill to the pub, arguing as we walked. We continued rowing throughout dinner. Finally

Susan said something I didn't quite hear and didn't think necessary to reply to.

She said, 'Oh, aren't we talking now?'

I replied, 'I didn't answer you because I didn't hear what you said but since you mention it I reckon it's a first-class idea if we don't talk. As we don't get on very well perhaps you'd like to mate up with somebody else!'

We finished our dinner in silence. Susan rose from the table and said, 'I'm going back to the hotel.'

I sat at the table feeling upset and eventually took a slow walk back. I went into the bar and ordered a pot of tea and climbed the stairs. Susan opened the door to my knock. As I walked across the room I saw she had been filling in a crossword puzzle. I placed the tray on the balcony table and sat on one of the chairs. I spent an hour or so watching the traffic. Eventually I returned to the room.

Susan said, 'I'm going to see the dolphins tomorrow. Would you like to come?'

I replied, 'No, thanks. I think I'll take a walk on the other side of the Rock.' The following day we went our separate ways and didn't meet up with each other until after dinner.

As I walked along the coast I came across a beautiful secluded bay which the other tourists hadn't discovered. I realized I had saved my holiday. I could happily spend the few mornings left sunbathing in the bay, attend some type of exhibition in the afternoon and go to a nearby restaurant where I would not be embarrassed to eat and I would still enjoy myself. I thought of Susan and her ruined holiday. When I saw her in the evening I said, 'I've found the most lovely little bay about twenty minutes' walk away. Would you like to go there tomorrow?'

She replied, 'Yes, all right, then.'

We sat on the concrete seats that encircled Rosario Bay making light conversation. We looked across the water to see Spain on the other side. To the west we could see the mountains of Morocco in the distance. Some time later we both had a paddle. I found the sea to be extremely cold and would not venture further. Susan plucked up courage and had a swim. She called out, 'Why don't you come in?'

I replied, 'I can't. The water's freezing. I've still got a stinking cold and I'm on antibiotics. If I go for a swim I'll catch pneumonia.' Fortunately the warm weather and the tablets had taken away the unpleasantness of my cold but I was interested in being healthy. Six times Susan invited me into the sea. I replied politely three times. The remaining three times I didn't answer. We returned to Rosario Bay the following morning and spent both afternoons visiting museums.

Although we were back on friendly terms I felt our relationship was strained. I made an effort not to reply to a few comments I thought untoward and I noticed Susan did the same. Despite this I still enjoyed my holiday.

On the last day of our stay we boarded one of the old buses that drive around Gibraltar. We paid the full fare and stayed on the bus until we returned to our pick-up point. Out of town the driver drove at speed and we would jump out of our seats as we travelled over the bumpy coastal roads.

In the evening we hired a taxi to drive us to the airport and found it considerably cheaper than the single transfer we had booked on our arrival. We had a good flight. There were no problems with the minicab. As we cleared customs we saw the driver holding a white placard with our names written on it. Susan and I chatted in the car. I was the first stop. I gave my half of the fare to the driver and said goodbye to Susan. She replied, 'Bye.'

Two days later I collected my photographs from the chemist. I saw a first-class photo of Susan sitting on top of a camel. I replaced the snaps in their holder thinking to myself, 'Susan would love that photograph, so post it to her.' But our disagreements were still in my mind. A week later I looked at the photos again. I thought, 'Don't be so unkind. Send her that photo.' I wrote a letter to Susan saying, 'I thought you might like this snap. If you have any of me could you send them through the post. I had a lovely holiday. I hope you did too. Best wishes, Sylvia.'

Three weeks passed by with no response from Susan. I realized this was intended as a slap in the face and yes, it did sting slightly. But it also made me think. I decided our rows must have seriously upset Susan and she had a lousy holiday. If that's right I'm sorry but it does take two to have an argument.

My opinion of Susan: I think she's very nice but she can be very argumentative and bad-tempered.

twenty-one

New York, USA

- 2001 -

10th September 2001

Canongate, my Scottish publishers, opened a publishing house in the city of New York, USA, and offered me a free trip there for one week in the month of September. They intended promoting their new branch and my book entitled *Misadventures*, which they had published in the UK earlier in the year and had decided to sell in the US. I accepted their invitation with great excitement. It was arranged that a journalist from a Scottish Sunday newspaper would travel to New York to show me the sights and get to know me and a photographer would take a lengthy photo-shoot. This would result in a 3,000–word story and a full front-page photograph of me in the paper's magazine. Coincidentally my agent, Caroline, was visiting New York on business at the time. She instructed her secretary to book her a seat on the plane I was travelling on and a room in the hotel I would be staying in. I eagerly looked forward to the trip.

On Thursday 6 September, I boarded a Boeing 747 airliner at two o'clock in the afternoon at Heathrow Airport bound for John F. Kennedy Airport, New York. Although I had looked around the departure lounge I had not seen Caroline. The plane was enormous. A stewardess told me it seated 450 passengers. It also had an upper floor containing a bar and spacious seating for business-class travellers. My seat was beside a window in the economy area towards the end of the aircraft. A young man sat in the seat beside me and an elderly American man occupied the aisle seat. Shortly after take-off Caroline appeared and told me she had nearly missed the plane as the boarding gate was further away than she had thought in the vast airport. She told me she was travelling in the business-class area.

The young man sitting beside me smiled at me and we were soon in conversation. He told me he was a Pakistani who lived in Karachi and he was on one month's holiday. He had spent fifteen days in London and intended spending the remaining fifteen days in New York. I noticed he wore a wedding ring on the small finger of his left hand. He looked in his mid-thirties and I assumed he had married in his twenties and was now divorced. He introduced himself as Ghumbo. I saw nothing wrong with chatting to another passenger as we flew across the Atlantic Ocean but unfortunately Ghumbo misunderstood my friendliness. I noticed he ran his tongue around his lips occasionally but I thought nothing of it until he lifted the dividing arm between our seats and moved closer to me. I quickly replaced the arm and wriggled out of his way. Some time later I decided to visit Caroline and said, 'Excuse me,' to Ghumbo as I left my seat. He did not move out of my way and I found myself squeezed against him whilst he placed his hands either side of my hips. I had a chat to Caroline and admired her spacious accommodation. I turned down her offer to swap seats and made my way back to the economy-class section. Ghumbo allowed me to pass him without touching me but as soon as I sat down he put his left arm on my right thigh and clutched my right knee. I replaced his arm on the seat divider and said, 'No, thank you,' and spent the remainder of the flight looking out of the window. Ghumbo did not speak to me again but began talking to the elderly American. I heard him say, 'I have a wife and three children in Karachi.'

The flight was smooth and lasted almost seven hours. I looked below us but we were high above thick clouds for most of the journey and I was unable to see through them.

Caroline and I met again as we passed through customs. Her blonde head stood out amongst the crowds. A young man wearing three-quarter-length trousers, sandals, a T-shirt and a baseball cap covering a shaven head walked up to me. Speaking with a light Scottish accent he said, 'Hello, Sylvia. I'm Colin from Canongate.' He shook hands with me whilst Caroline introduced herself. I realized he had recognized me from photographs available in the publisher's office. He led us out of the airport and hailed a yellow cab and accompanied us to our hotel.

The hotel was situated in a side street of Manhattan on the edge of a small square with a park in its centre. It looked extremely promising with its long canopy that stretched from the main entrance across the pavement to the kerb. Colin dealt with reception and told me he and a journalist named Anna would call for me at ten fifteen the next morning. He gave me his telephone number and left the hotel. Caroline and I were allotted two rooms on the third floor of the eighteen-storey building. I was very pleased with my accommodation. My room was huge and contained a double bed, two desks, an armchair and a large coloured TV on a stand. Various doors led into a bathroom, a small kitchen and two walk-in wardrobes, one of which had a full-length mirror on its front and a lockable wall safe inside it. Caroline's room was much smaller and minus a kitchen. We unpacked and dined together in the dining hall on the ground floor. It was now 8 p.m. in New York but 1 a.m. in the UK as there is a time difference of five hours between the two countries. We were both very tired and went to bed soon after we had eaten.

I woke shortly before 7 a.m. New York time and found I was very thirsty. There were no tea- or coffee-making facilities in my room so I telephoned room service requesting a hot drink. I was told there were no morning drinks until the dining room opened at 7.30 a.m. and that there were no vending machines in the hotel either. I was very annoyed. I dressed and went down to reception to see if I could alter the situation. I was told there was nothing they could do. I asked to speak to the manager and was advised that he would arrive at 8 a.m. I returned to my room and decided to have a bath. I turned on the hot tap to find brown-coloured water gushing from it. I had a shower instead and noticed how hot the water was. I saw grubby footprints ground into the floor of the bath. At eight fifteen I returned to reception and voiced my complaint to the manager. He replied, 'This is a Union hotel and our rules are that the restaurant doesn't open until seven thirty. If you want tea or coffee before then you should take a walk around the block and use one of the facilities that are open at that time.' I was amazed by his answer. Rather than lose the battle completely I told him of the dirty footmarks at the bottom of the bath and how brown water gushed from its tap. He replied, 'There are some roadworks under way at the moment and hopefully when these are completed in a few days' time the water will clear. But I can certainly have the bath cleaned for you.'

I tried the bath water daily but its colour didn't alter. I decided to shower instead but I soon found a problem with that too. I was unable to merge the cold- and hot-water taps to provide warm water. I would turn both taps on at the same time, then test the temperature and climb into the bath and step underneath the shower when it was warm, only to find the water became so hot it hurt me. I would quickly jump out of the bath, and turn the hot tap off leaving the cold tap running. When the temperature cooled down I would step under the shower again until the water slowly became too cold to use. My daily routine of jumping in and out of the shower angered me.

I soon discovered a problem with the long thick paper blinds that hung under the venetian blinds at the windows. At the end of each day I would close the venetian blinds and pull the paper ones down. After I'd showered in the mornings I would hoist the venetian blinds halfway up the window. I would then quickly tug and release the paper blinds in the hope that they would rise a few feet. Instead they would either hang almost to the floor or noisily rush to the ceiling. I would return to my room later in the day to find the maid had sorted out my problem.

To my amusement throughout my stay I lost four room keys, each time in my room. Reception politely supplied me with spares. I managed to locate three of the missing keys.

Caroline had none of these problems. She was quite happy to wait for a hot drink but as the days passed she found her telephone was losing half its messages so she asked reception to find her other accommodation with a reliable telephone. She was given a beautiful non-smoking room on the fifteenth floor. Expensive net curtains hung at the windows and a cream carpet covered the floor. Caroline was kept very busy visiting New York publishers to promote her clients' books. We usually met at nine thirty each morning and breakfasted together, discussing our varying days. In her absence she would leave telephone messages on my answerphone.

Colin escorted Anna to the hotel for our ten fifteen meeting. She joined Caroline and me at the breakfast table whilst he returned to his office. Anna was a Scot. She was slim with short dark hair and in her mid-thirties. We discussed where she would take me. Caroline suggested, 'Well, you must have shopping to do, so why don't you visit the famous store Bloomingdales?' As I had eight presents to buy I thought that was a good idea. Anna agreed. She told me she had stayed in New York many times before and knew her way around the city. Anna and I left the hotel and hired a yellow cab. As we journeyed through New York for the first time in my life I saw skyscrapers. I had to lower my head in the back of the cab to see the tops of them. We arrived at Bloomingdales and discovered they had a sale on. I shopped in the souvenir department and managed to buy five presents at half their original prices, whilst Anna bought three summer tops at a reduced rate in the clothing department. I brought my three remaining presents in sales elsewhere in the city.

After lunch in the store our next stop was Central Park. I was surprised to find a small zoo at its entrance. We decided to go into it. We walked around the enclosures in the hot sun. It seemed to be a children's zoo filled with lizards, penguins and seals. The only dangerous animal I saw was a large polar bear who was swimming on his back in his pool. A pigeon landed on the rocks slightly above his head. I watched as he lashed out with one of his giant paws and grabbed the pigeon. The bird managed to fly away with its wings intact but minus quite a few long tail feathers. Anna and I sat on the benches outside the zoo quietly chatting and observing the other tourists.

I enjoyed sightseeing with Anna. We travelled on the subway and in yellow cabs, splitting our expenses. The weather was very hot and sunny. She told me New York was unbearably hot in June. At lunch she asked me if I'd like to try her iced tea. I did. It tasted like cold rhubarb. I spent an afternoon with Anna, Colin and two of their friends. We walked across the Brooklyn Bridge and saw the twin towers of the World Trade Center in the distance. We also walked through Chinatown with its gay shops selling their gaudy wares.

Anna treated me to lunch in an expensive restaurant. After our meal we travelled to the Staten Island Ferry where we met up with a young Scottish photographer named Stewart, and began a three-hour photo-shoot. Stewart snapped me in various poses inside the boat and on deck as we sailed across the water. Some of the passengers watched us out of curiosity. Others did their best to ignore us. As we disembarked we saw two policemen watching the crowds. Stewart persuaded one of them to be photographed with me and told him he would be famous in Scotland. I was also photographed in the subway and getting in and out of a yellow cab.

Caroline had a day free so we decided to journey on the ferry to see the Statue of Liberty, which sat on an island in New York Harbour. It was a glorious day. We decided not to climb inside the statue as it was far too high. We chose to walk around it. I heard English accents coming from the crowds. In the afternoon we visited the Metropolitan Museum and lunched in its rooftop cafe with its magnificent views over Central Park and the Manhattan sky-scrapers.

I found New York quite exciting. I liked the way I discovered leafy parks amongst the buildings. But I didn't like the yellow cabs as they were simply four-door cars where the passengers squeezed into the back seat and were partitioned from the driver. I much preferred the spacious London taxis. I found the policemen to be extremely friendly and helpful to me and I particularly liked the law that decreed all dogs should be walked on a lead, and the absence of stray dogs roaming the city. I also appreciated how clean the streets were. I noted there were few supermarkets and was told that New Yorkers usually eat out in the many restaurants after a day's work. I thought the lack of public toilets in the streets a good idea. They were found in cafes and bars but they appeared to be badly erected, usually revealing the occupant in the cubicle. Phoning London was extremely cheap. I paid $10 for a phone card and was able to speak to my mother each day for several minutes for an entire week. It seemed to me that Americans put sugar in every-thing, including mushroom soup and red cabbage. There was a plentiful supply of bookshops so I decided New Yorkers must be avid readers.

Tuesday 11 September 2001

At 7.45 a.m. New York time my friend Leslie telephoned me from London, interrupting my sleep. He
had phoned twice before, leaving messages on the
answerphone in my absence. This time he phoned
in his lunch hour when he knew it would be early
morning in New York. We chatted for a few
minutes, discussing the cold and wet weather in
London and how hot it was in New York, and
how my elderly widowed mother was faring as he
phoned her daily as a double check for her welfare.
He ended the call by saying he would see me soon
as I was due to return to London the following day.
As I was now wide awake I drank the fruit juice I
had stored in my refrigerator and then showered
and dressed. At 9.15 a.m. Caroline knocked on my
door and said, 'I've been out walking and I think
there's been a bad accident at the World Trade
Center. Apparently a plane has hit it.' We turned
the television on and discovered that at 8.45 a.m. a
commercial airliner with passengers on board had
flown into one of the twin towers of the World

Trade Center in Lower Manhattan. And eighteen minutes later another commercial airliner, again with passengers on board, had flown into the remaining tower. Caroline and I gasped at the horror unfolding on the screen. Both towers were 110 storeys high and full with employees beginning their working day and now the towers were on fire. Eventually I went down to breakfast and Caroline left the hotel to keep her many appointments. As I passed the bar opposite reception and next door to the dining hall I saw it was full of people watching the hotel's huge TV screen. Everyone was talking about the disaster and several women were in tears. When I returned to my room I switched on the TV and found that whilst I had been eating my breakfast the two towers had collapsed, a third commercial airliner with passengers on board had crashed into the Pentagon and a fourth commercial airliner, again with passengers on board, had crashed into the countryside near Pittsburgh. It was reported that these were terrorist attacks with suicide pilots at the controls. The opinion was that the fourth airliner was intended to damage the White House. The hotel I was staying in was only one mile away from the World Trade Center.

I realized my mother would see these atrocities

on British TV. I tried to phone her but all the lines were busy and it was 4 p.m. New York time before I was able to speak to her. She was in tears but very relieved to hear I was unharmed.

Two days previously I had watched a current-affairs programme on New York TV and had seen the lovely Barbara Olson, a Federal Prosecutor and celebrity, answer viewers' questions. A newsreader stated that Mrs Olson had been on board the plane that had crashed into the Pentagon. We were told that shortly before the crash she had locked herself in the toilet and used her mobile phone to speak to her husband, telling him the plane was being hijacked and asking him, 'What do I do?' She was forty-five years old and very happily married. She lost her life a few minutes later.

I chose to spend the remainder of Tuesday in the hotel watching TV in my room. The newsreader stated that President Bush had ordered all the airports to be closed over the entire country. Airborne planes were instructed to land immediately or divert to Canada and all future flights were cancelled until the authorities had control of the situation. I was due to fly home the following morning. Quite obviously I was unable to. I went downstairs to reception and spoke to the manager, telling him I would not be able to leave until there was a plane available. He smiled and replied, 'Then you have to stay with us until then.' I returned to my room and the TV set. The newsreader told us warships were in the harbour and military jets were flying over the city. I could see the jets from my bedroom window. I walked to the corner of the street and saw dense smoke filling the sky over what had been the World Trade Center. We were to smell smoke for several days and became used to the sound of sirens of the emergency services. All roads in Manhattan were closed to general traffic.

On the Wednesday I bought a newspaper from the hotel shop and saw photographs of people hanging out the windows of the twin towers and of others jumping to their deaths as they tried to escape the inferno within the building, just before the two towers collapsed.

There was still a problem with the telephones but I was finally able to speak to Colin, who told me the company would continue to pay my hotel bill. I managed to speak to my mother daily. She was very upset and very concerned for my wellbeing.

On the Thursday morning just after 9 a.m. Caroline knocked on my door. She told me she had been out in the streets and had seen Bill Clinton. She said, 'I was so close to him I could have spoken to him but I didn't try because I thought other people might need to. But I did take a few photographs of him.'

During the day I busied myself visiting bookshops and had lunch in a cafe, being careful not to lose my way as there were no yellow cabs to rescue me. In the evening I dined with Caroline in the hotel. I commented, 'The bread is stale.'

She replied, 'That's because the food trucks can't get into Manhattan.'

Caroline told me she had tried to give blood but there was such a long queue she felt they didn't need hers. She was due to fly home the following morning. We decided that if ever there was a problem with hotel rooms we could always share each other's.

All the many TV stations were focused on the atrocity for several days. One station concentrated on finding missing people. Relatives would appear on the screen clutching photographs, giving out names and asking for information about their loved ones with their telephone number displayed at the bottom of the screen. Most of them were fighting back tears. It was terribly, terribly sad. In total over 3,000 people died in the atrocity. President Bush declared it 'an act of war' and later visited the city against the advice of his Secret Service men.

I did experience an uneasy three days. I wondered if the atrocity was a 'one-off' or if there was more to come. But as time passed by I considered it was a terrorist attack that would not be attempted again for at least several weeks. I walked through the streets of New York at ease, as did Caroline. Everybody behaved in a normal manner and went about life as they usually did. I did not see any panic. Anna, the journalist, very kindly phoned me to make sure I was safe.

Caroline and I noticed an empty police car that had been parked for some days on the edge of the square. We hoped the policeman was safe.

Caroline and I had brought sufficient clothing for our stay but as the days passed we ran into minor problems. First of all I have to have medication every day and I was running out of tablets and in need of more. Plus we both had a machineload of dirty washing to clean. Caroline solved our problems. She said to me, 'I have some lovely friends in the countryside just outside New York. They're very old friends of mine called Clare and Bruce and Bruce is a retired doctor. I've just phoned them and we have an invite to lunch. Bruce said he can write you out a prescription and we can borrow their washing machine. I told them your problems with your bathroom and they said you can have a bath too if you want.' This certainly solved my immediate problems and a bath sounded lovely as my bath water was as brown as ever and I was tired of jumping in and out of my shower. We hired a yellow cab to take us to the train station and bought return tickets to and from the village of Plandome, a half-hour train ride from the city. Bruce met us at the station. Clare and Bruce were both elderly.

Clare provided an excellent ham-salad lunch which we ate as the washing machine worked to clean our clothing. I saw brightly coloured birds mingling with sparrows as they ate from the bird table in the vast garden. The house was detached and spacious with a veranda and lawns all the way round it. We were surrounded by similar homes. I saw a swimming pool glistening under the trees. Bruce very kindly wrote out a prescription then drove me to the local pharmacy where I paid approximately £25 for the tablets. On our return he showed me the Sound. It was a large boating marina that led to the open sea and it was beautiful. We walked across the sand and he presented me with a clamshell. There were many white-painted piers and I noticed houses set amongst the trees lining the waterway. On our return to the house I had a hot bath. I particularly noticed clean sparkling water coming out of the taps. At the end of the afternoon we collected the washing that Clare had dried in her drier and Bruce returned us to the train station. I had spent a pleasant afternoon in first-class company.

After breakfast the following day I decided to visit the local shops. I entered a bank and obtained more dollars for my extended stay. After lunch in one of the cafes I chose to read a book in the park adjacent to the hotel. I asked reception if I could do so as the park was locked to keep out passers-by. Ben the doorman appeared with a large key on a huge metal key ring. We walked along the railings and he unlocked one of the gates, saying, 'I'll collect you in an hour's time.' I walked around the park. It was quite small but well cared for with evergreens ornately cut. There were many benches bearing nameplates of late residents of the square. I saw several squirrels running around and noticed they climbed to the very tops of the high trees. There were a few elderly ladies sitting on the benches and several nannies with their young charges. After inspecting the flowerbeds I settled down to my book. I notice an hour had passed without any sign of Ben. Approximately half an hour later, and still no sign of Ben, I saw some of the nannies unlock a gate to take the children home. I slipped through them and returned to the hotel. I asked the relief doorman, 'Where is Ben?'

He replied, 'He went home some time ago.'

I asked, 'Didn't he tell you to let me out of the park?'

'No,' he replied.

All the waiters in the hotel dining room were extremely polite and attentive to their diners. A plump middle-aged waiter named Raimond made it clear he found me very attractive. When he attended my table, instead of looking me straight in the eye, he would look at my bosom and talk with a smile on his face. At other times he would wink and make faces at me. In return I would laugh because I found him to be extremely funny. But his continuing admiring looks at my bosom offended me and I sensed his attentions were heading in the wrong direction. I decided to ignore him in an attempt to quash his ardour. The next mealtime I did not look at Raimond but from the corner of my eye I could see him watching me. When my dinner was served he walked up to my table. Looking appreciatively at my bosom again he asked, 'Would you like some pepper, madam?'

I replied, 'Yes, please.'

He picked up the large peppershaker from the main table. He shook it and twisted it into several provocative positions.

I thought it so funny I was unable to control my laughter. As he sprinkled pepper over my plate he said, 'I have some work to do in the hotel this evening. I will be staying in room 329.' I made no comment but realized he saw my room number on the docket I signed every mealtime. Room 329 was four doors away from mine. I left the restaurant without a backward glance and returned to my room. As the door was self-locking I usually put the safety chain on only but this time I turned the extra lock. I changed into my nightwear and settled down to watch television. Before I went to bed I locked both my bathroom and bedroom windows although I did not expect the portly Raimond to climb a ladder from the lower roof and squeeze through either window. I thought to myself, 'If he knocks on my door I'll just tell him to go away and if that fails all I have to do is pick up the telephone receiver and dial 0 for the switchboard operator behind reception.' But my mind ran away with me. I wondered if Raimond was freshly showered and doused in cologne laying on his bed in his Y-fronts with his hands behind his head waiting for me. I wondered what his reaction would be when he realized I was not going to appear. I closed my eyes and went to sleep. There was no knock to disturb my slumber. I went down to breakfast with Caroline at nine thirty the following morning, curious to see Raimond's reaction. I noticed he looked at me but he did not approach our table. In the evening I went to dinner by myself. Raimond was standing in the entrance of the dining hall. He smiled at me and said, 'Good evening, madam. Please allow me to escort you to your table.' He hooked his left arm in invitation. I slipped my arm through his and he led me to a vacant table. He was extremely polite and friendly towards me and he looked me straight in the eye when he spoke to me.

Caroline decided to travel to Boston where she had business contacts and stay two nights. She said to me, 'There are some marvellous art galleries there and I'd like to see some paintings.' We were unable to book plane seats as although the airports had reopened there was a queue for seats. After Caroline left the hotel Colin phoned me and said, 'I've booked you on a plane tomorrow morning at 8.25

a.m. I'll see you in the hotel bar tonight about seven thirty and I'll give you all the details.' I was very pleased and packed immediately. I didn't have a telephone number to contact Caroline so I was unable to speak to her. Colin arrived at the hotel as arranged accompanied by Anna and his friend Dave. He told me, 'One of your friends phoned Edinburgh today to see if you were OK.' I was very touched. He paid my hotel bill by credit card and I booked a cab to arrive at 3 a.m. to take me to John F. Kennedy Airport. We spent the remainder of the evening talking in the bar. I was the first of our party to return to the UK.

I sat on the plane, relieved to be going home at last. I looked around me and was surprised to see four empty seats as people were desperate to return to London. As we flew away from New York I remembered Caroline's last telephone message to me which had ended, 'What a great adventure we have shared together, Sylvia.'